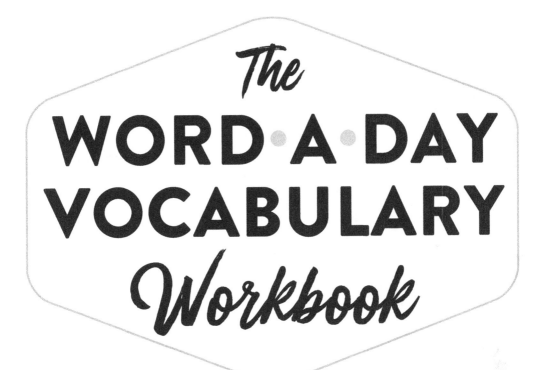

The WORD·A·DAY VOCABULARY Workbook

Sound Smarter, Write Better— One Day at a Time!

Francine Puckly

T0019391

Adams Media
New York   London   Toronto   Sydney   New Delhi

FOR DEAN—
I couldn't have done it without you!

Adams Media
An Imprint of Simon & Schuster, LLC
100 Technology Center Drive
Stoughton, MA 02072

First Adams Media trade paperback edition January 2021

ADAMS MEDIA and colophon are trademarks of Simon & Schuster, LLC.

For information about special discounts for bulk purchases, please contact Simon & Schuster Special Sales at 1-866-506-1949 or business@simonandschuster.com.

The Simon & Schuster Speakers Bureau can bring authors to your live event. For more information or to book an event contact the Simon & Schuster Speakers Bureau at 1-866-248-3049 or visit our website at www.simonspeakers.com.

Interior design by Julia Jacintho

Manufactured in the United States of America

3 2024

Library of Congress Cataloging-in-Publication Data has been applied for.

ISBN 978-1-5072-1569-2

Contains material adapted from the following title published by Adams Media, an Imprint of Simon & Schuster, LLC: *The Big Book of Words You Should Know* by David Olsen, Michelle Bevilacqua, and Justin Cord Hayes, copyright © 2009, ISBN 978-1-60550-139-0.

CONTENTS

INTRODUCTION

Do you know what **apostate**, **execrable**, and **potage** mean? What about **waggish**, **flibbertigibbet**, and **contumelious**? As you study, write, and use words such as these, you'll find yourself stunned at the complexity and flexibility of the English language. Throughout the centuries, it has borrowed, adapted, and created out of whole cloth more than 270,000 words. With the assistance of your invaluable guide, *The Word-a-Day Vocabulary Workbook*, you can learn and enjoy more of them.

As you work through the book's writing prompts that accompany each of its 367 words, you'll learn to make them a part of your everyday vocabulary.

You'll find prompts such as:

- **LOGY**: Write a short scene or paragraph incorporating *logy*, *weather*, *Julie*, and *fireplace*.

- **FREEBOOTER**: What are five ways a person could be a *freebooter*?

- **BEHEMOTH**: Finish the scene using *behemoth*: John wrestled with the grill, trying to get it off the back of his pickup truck. It had taken three men to load the grill but, for some reason, he thought he could unload it by himself...

The prompts range from using the word in a sentence or writing a paragraph or two to making a list of people or things that are examples of the word.

Each entry in this book includes a word (often unusual), how to pronounce it, its part of speech, its definition, and an example of its usage. There's also some back-story or trivia about the word and a writing prompt. If you work through the book, doing one word a day, within a year you'll have a new and improved vocabulary!

Let us commence! Start your **edification** by absorbing a new word today. Your friends will **lionize** you!

ENIGMATICAL
(en-egg-MA-ti-kul), adjective

Unclear in meaning; open to more than one interpretation.

EXAMPLE:

The letter from my mother was **ENIGMATICAL** as to the date of the family reunion, so we'll have to call her to get the specifics.

TRIVIA:

The root word *enigmatic* originated in the seventeenth century and derives from the Greek word *ainigma*, meaning "riddle."

MAKE IT STICK:

Incorporating the word *enigmatical,* write a brief synopsis for a mystery that Sherlock Holmes and his trusty sidekick John Watson must unravel.

_____
_____
_____
_____
_____
_____
_____
_____

KOWTOW
(KOW-tow), verb

To show respect, deference, or servility.

EXAMPLE:

For the sake of keeping peace in the family, Alice **KOWTOWED** to her father, spending her evenings at home instead of joining her friends at the club.

TRIVIA:

Kowtow's origin comes from the Chinese custom of kneeling and touching one's forehead to the ground as an expression of respect or deference. Kowtowing isn't necessarily backing down, but the word has taken on that connotation in its English usage.

MAKE IT STICK:

What's one decision you've made in life where you regretted *kowtowing* to someone else's authority?

_____
_____
_____
_____
_____
_____

IMPASTO
(im-PAHS-toe), noun

Paint that has been laid thickly on a canvas as with a palette knife.

EXAMPLE:

"By 1887, Vincent van Gogh abandoned heavy **IMPASTO** and reveled in an impressive range of dots and dashes, lattice lines, and basket-weave patterns."
—Michael Kimmelman, art critic

MAKE IT STICK:

Using the word *impasto*, write about a painting you admire.

TRIVIA:

Impasto refers to paint applied thickly to canvas in order to make it stand out from the surface. The technique was first used by Venetian Renaissance artists Titian and Tintoretto and in the seventeenth century by Baroque painters Rembrandt and Rubens, but perhaps the most famous impasto painting is *Starry Night* by Vincent van Gogh. His use of the impasto technique gives viewers the feeling that the sky is actually moving.

FRANGIBLE
(FRAN-juh-bull), adjective

Easily breakable.

TRIVIA:

Holding its early fifteenth-century meaning of "easily breakable," *frangible* usually refers to delicate items, but pie crusts, thin crackers, and emotions can also be frangible, though these uses are less common. Bullets designed to disintegrate into tiny particles upon impact are called frangible bullets.

MAKE IT STICK:

Write a scene incorporating the words *frangible, merlot,* and *snatch.*

ABECEDARIAN
(ay-bee-see-DARE-ee-un), noun

A beginner; someone just learning the rudiments of a task, skill, job, etc.

EXAMPLE:

Paul is an expert in a sea kayak, but when it comes to snow skiing, he's an **ABECEDARIAN**.

TRIVIA:

From Medieval Latin *abecedārium*, it refers to the initial knowledge or "ABCs" of a skill or task. Abecedarian is also a poetic form in which a line or stanza begins with the first letter of the alphabet and subsequent lines or stanzas begin with successive letters of the alphabet.

MAKE IT STICK:

Write a poem using the *abecedarian* format.

PASQUINADE
(pas-kwi-NAYD), noun

A grotesquely or absurdly exaggerated representation (think political cartoons).

EXAMPLE:

The paintings of Toulouse-Lautrec are often rooted in **PASQUINADE** but are more than mere cartoons.

TRIVIA:

In their music video for "Land of Confusion," the band members of Genesis are represented by puppet pasquinades. Fittingly, notable politicians are also often depicted in this manner.

MAKE IT STICK:

Using *pasquinade*, describe what a drawing of your favorite political candidate would look like.

TOADY
(TOE-dee), noun

Someone with a slavish devotion to a person in power.

EXAMPLE:

Sheila ducked into the ladies' room when she saw Sandra and all her **TOADIES** heading across the office.

TRIVIA:

The word *toady* first appeared at the end of the seventeenth century.

MAKE IT STICK:

What are five things you would never do again if you had *toadies* to do them for you?

1. _____
_____

2. _____
_____

3. _____
_____

4. _____
_____

5. _____
_____

AU CONTRAIRE
(oh kon-TRARE), noun

On the contrary; the opposite.

EXAMPLE:

"AU CONTRAIRE, you pompous fool," cried Jeanne. "I'm not playing hard to get at all, but rather despise you with all my heart!"

TRIVIA:

This phrase is lifted directly from the French language: *au*, meaning "to the," and *contraire*, meaning "contrary."

MAKE IT STICK:

Write out a disagreement you might have with a family member, using *au contraire* in your dialogue.

_____
_____
_____
_____
_____
_____
_____
_____
_____
_____
_____
_____

COMITY
(KOM-ih-tee), noun

Courtesy; mutual civility.

EXAMPLE:

The police were kind enough to grant me the **COMITY** of a private telephone call once I promised to stop removing articles of clothing and flinging them at the sergeant.

TRIVIA:

Comity typically refers to the civility or courtesy exercised between people, organizations, and nations and has retained its early English meaning from the 1540s. The phrase "comity of nations" was coined in 1812 and refers to the mutual respect for each nation's laws and institutions.

MAKE IT STICK:

Write a scene in which *comity* is granted to your character after he/she is placed in an embarrassing situation.

QUIESCENT
(kwee-ESS-unt), adjective

Dormant; inactive.

EXAMPLE:

The **QUIESCENT** old piano that once rang out triumph after triumph has been standing in its oak-paneled room since the day of its master's death.

TRIVIA:

Abraham Lincoln said, "Great distance in either time or space has wonderful power to lull and render quiescent the human mind." This gets harder and harder to do in a world of constant contact, but it's a wise observation indeed.

MAKE IT STICK:

Using *quiescent,* describe three things that are dormant or inactive in your life or surroundings.

_____
_____
_____
_____
_____
_____
_____

JOCOSE
(joh-KOHSS), adjective

Characterized by joking and good humor.

EXAMPLE:

Everyone loves Bob because of his **JOCOSE** manner.

TRIVIA:

From the 1670s (perhaps from a court jester) and related to jocular. Both *jocose* and *jocular* imply a fondness for merry-making and joking.

MAKE IT STICK:

Using *jocose,* describe a friend or family member who is always full of good humor.

_____
_____
_____
_____
_____
_____
_____
_____
_____
_____

QUIETUS
(kwhy-EAT-us), noun

**Something that ends or settles a situation;
death or retirement.**

EXAMPLE:

The **QUIETUS** of the argument
arrived when Marteeka made a point
Frieda could not refute.

TRIVIA:

Quietus is a poetic, old-fashioned
word for "death"—in particular,
death that is seen as a relief or
eternal rest, as was the case in
Shakespeare's famous "To be, or not
to be" soliloquy in *Hamlet*. It's also
the death of a disagreement!

MAKE IT STICK:

You're standing at the ticket counter at Los Angeles International
Airport trying to convince the customer service employee to put you
on the next flight to Boston. Describe how the rest of this scene plays out,
including the *quietus,* or how the situation is settled.

DONNYBROOK

(DAHN-ee-brook), noun

A free-for-all, knock-down, drag-out fight.

EXAMPLE:

Police expected a **DONNYBROOK** at the protest march, but both those for and against the issue were peaceful and courteous.

MAKE IT STICK:

Describe a bench-clearing brawl at a hockey or basketball game. Who's involved and how does it get back under control? Be sure to use the word *donnybrook*.

TRIVIA:

Hockey is well known for its bench-clearing brawls, and the term *donnybrook* remains well known today thanks to Chuck Brodsky's "Hockey Fight Song." The word, however, has its roots in Ireland, not Canada. In 1204, King John of England granted a license to Dublin to hold an eight-day fair in its suburb of Donnybrook. The fair was held annually for over six hundred years but morphed from a proper fair into an affair of drunken debauchery. It took some finagling, but the license was finally sold away from the town and the fair abolished in the mid-1800s.

GALOOT
(guh-LOOT), noun

An eccentric or foolish person.

EXAMPLE:

Mike's outdated clothes and hairstyle cause many to consider him a **GALOOT.**

TRIVIA:

This term was made famous by Yosemite Sam in his referring to Bugs Bunny as a "long-eared galoot!"

MAKE IT STICK:

Use the words *galoot, pop-bottle glasses, plaid,* and *stripes* to describe a person.

CONTRABAND
(KAHN-truh-band), noun

Illegal or prohibited goods.

EXAMPLE:

Emily tried to smuggle a tape recorder into the concert but her **CONTRABAND** was quickly discovered and taken from her.

TRIVIA:

The word literally means "against the ban," and the first reference of it pertaining to smuggled goods was in the 1590s. Did you know hand sanitizer is considered contraband in all federal prisons as well as twelve state prisons?

MAKE IT STICK:

Incorporating the word **contraband,** describe a scenario where someone smuggles fireworks into a state in which they're illegal.

SPURIOUS
(SPUR-ee-us), adjective

Fake; counterfeit.

TRIVIA:

The word in its current usage dates from the late sixteenth century and was first applied to false marriages. It had been occasionally used as a name for the offspring of illegitimate relationships, though without any stigma (Spurius Lucretius Tricipitinus, for instance, was made a temporary magistrate of Rome). It derives from the Latin *spurius*, meaning "false."

MAKE IT STICK:

Write a scene in which a racehorse has *spurious* pedigree papers.

PARSIMONIOUS
(par-suh-MOAN-ee-uss), adjective

Stingy; exceptionally frugal or thrifty.

TRIVIA:

Though not necessarily negative in its 1590s meaning of "very sparing in expenditure," *parsimonious* shifted to meaning "stinginess" in the eighteenth century.

MAKE IT STICK:

Finish this scene incorporating the word *parsimonious*:
Helen sat in stunned silence as her mother's will was read.

CONSECRATE
(KON-si-krate), verb

To proclaim as sacred; to set aside or declare to be holy. By extension, to commit to something with a conviction in keeping with strong faith.

EXAMPLE:

Jean **CONSECRATED** her Tuesday morning writing date; she does not miss it for any reason.

TRIVIA:

While Abraham Lincoln's Gettysburg Address stated that we cannot consecrate the battlefield, his famous and moving speech effectively did just that.

MAKE IT STICK:

List five goals you have committed to and *consecrated*.

1. _____

2. _____

3. _____

4. _____

5. _____

KISMET
(KIZ-mut), noun

The idea that current circumstances result from one's past actions, decisions, or lifestyle; consequences of one's past.

EXAMPLE:

Greg put his car trouble down to the bad automotive **KISMET**.

TRIVIA:

The word *kismet* was borrowed from the Turks in the nineteenth century. Ultimately, it comes from the Arabic word *qisma*, which means "lot."

MAKE IT STICK:

Write a short paragraph incorporating *kismet*, *book*, *Donna*, and *marshmallows*.

_____
_____
_____
_____
_____
_____
_____
_____
_____
_____
_____
_____

LICENTIOUS
(ly-SEN-shus), adjective

Without moral discretion or standards; to act as though the distinctions of right and wrong are nonexistent; entirely focused on one's own pleasure.

EXAMPLE:

Ancient Romans, toward the end of the empire's reign, ceased to maintain their borders and devoted themselves to **LICENTIOUS** behavior.

TRIVIA:

Unsurprisingly, given their behavior, the Romans coined the word *licentia*, from which we derive *licentious*. Although often applied to irresponsible sexual behavior, it does have a broader meaning. While the word *license*, which has the same root, can simply mean "permission" or "freedom," *licentious* almost always means "a license taken too far."

MAKE IT STICK:

Talk about three things you feel are *licentious* in nature.

1. _____

_____

_____

2. _____

_____

_____

3. _____

_____

_____

ROTE

(roat), noun

A habit or mechanical routine.

EXAMPLE:

The children learned their multiplication tables by **ROTE**.

TRIVIA:

From around 1300, *rote* means "custom" and "habit," and the phrase *bi rote* means "by heart." There is much debate as to whether rote learning is as effective as other learning methods.

MAKE IT STICK:

Write down three things you have learned by *rote*.

1. _____

_____

2. _____

_____

3. _____

_____

LAPIDARY

(LA-pih-dar-ee), adjective

Having to do with stones, specifically, their polishing, carving, and engraving.

EXAMPLE:

In his shop on Main Street, Russell showed passersby his **LAPIDARY** skills.

TRIVIA:

The Latin for "stone" is *lapis*, so it's not too surprising that in the 1400s, people began applying the word *lapidary* to the work of jewelers and others who worked with decorative stone. A jewel cutter's workshop might be referred to as a lapidarium.

MAKE IT STICK:

Describe, using the word *lapidary*, a piece of jewelry of which you're very fond. Tell how you got it and what it means to you.

_____

_____

_____

_____

_____

_____

_____

_____

QUERULOUS
(KWER-uh-luss), adjective

Given to complaining; habitually making peevish complaints.

EXAMPLE:

Adrienne, a **QUERULOUS** young woman, complained about all her problems during lunch at work.

TRIVIA:

Arriving on the scene around 1400 and taken from Old French *querelos*, meaning "quarrelsome, argumentative," and Latin *querulous*, meaning "full of complaints, complaining," *querulous* shares its roots with *quarrel*.

MAKE IT STICK:

Using the word *querulous*, finish the scene:
Margaret stared at the dinner the waiter slid in front of her...

_____

_____

_____

_____

_____

_____

_____

_____

_____

_____

_____

_____

_____

_____

QUAHOG
(KO-hog), noun

An edible clam found off the Atlantic coast of North America.

TRIVIA:

Roger Williams was a Puritan minister, theologian, author, abolitionist, and staunch advocate for religious freedom and the separation of church and state. He is credited with bringing *quahog* into the English language from the Narragansett *poquaûhock* or Pequot *p'quaghhaug*, meaning "hard clam." The quahog is used in New England clam chowder.

MAKE IT STICK:

Write a scene in which you or a character of your choosing is entering a New England clam chowder contest. Use the word *quahog*.

BROUHAHA
(BROO-ha-ha), noun

An event that involves or invokes excitement, turmoil, or conflict.

TRIVIA:

A brouhaha is marked by a confused state and much fuss (and may include loud noises coming from different directions). Oftentimes, in hindsight, the fuss was pointless or irrational. Families might make a brouhaha about holiday celebrations, fans might become overly excited about spotting a celebrity walking down the street, and a bench-clearing fight at a baseball game might be triggered by a simple misunderstanding.

MAKE IT STICK:

Describe a chaotic street scene using *brouhaha*. What caused the brouhaha? What are some of the people doing?

ARDUOUS
(AR-joo-us), adjective

Requiring exceptional effort or care; mentally or physically challenging; pushing limits.

EXAMPLE:

Stacy has been preparing all week for the **ARDUOUS** marathon competition.

TRIVIA:

Princess Anne, only daughter of Queen Elizabeth II and Prince Phillip, once stated, "Golf seems to be an arduous way to go for a walk. I prefer to take the dogs out."

MAKE IT STICK:

Write two sentences using the word *arduous*, first as something mentally challenging and then as something physically challenging.

1. _____

_____

_____

2. _____

_____

_____

DENIGRATE
(DEH-nih-grate), verb

To defame or slander.

EXAMPLE:

My opponent's ceaseless attempts to **DENIGRATE** me during this campaign reached a new low when she accused me of being on the side of the neo-Nazi movement.

TRIVIA:

First used in the sixteenth century, the word's roots lie in the Latin *denigrare*, meaning "to blacken."

MAKE IT STICK:

Using *denigrate*, write about a recent story you read or saw that slandered an individual.

_____

_____

_____

_____

_____

_____

_____

_____

_____

_____

_____

DREGS
(dreggs), noun

Literally refers to the (sediment-bearing) contents at the
bottom of a nearly empty container of wine, coffee, or the like;
something or someone perceived as worthless
or as the last and least appealing in a series of choices.

EXAMPLE:

Though many in her town looked on ex-convicts as the **DREGS** of society, it was Debbie's job as a social worker to try to rehabilitate everyone who came through her door, regardless of their history.

TRIVIA:

When jazz-fusion band Dixie Grit broke up, two members continued on as a duet, calling themselves the Dixie Dregs. Literally, this means the "sediment at the bottom" or the "least-wanted portion," but figuratively it can also mean the "small amount left," so the Dixie Dregs can be considered the small amount left of the band. Since they are incredibly skilled musicians, they are certainly not the least-wanted portion of the original band.

MAKE IT STICK:

Write a short paragraph using *dregs, coffee, waitress,* and *tip.*

OSTENTATIOUS

(oss-ten-TAY-shuss), adjective

Showy; seeking attention with gaudy displays of talents or possessions.

EXAMPLE:

You shouldn't take the Rolls to the party; it will be seen as **OSTENTATIOUS**.

TRIVIA:

Originating from the Latin word *ostentare*, meaning "to display," the modern English interpretation grew into "showy, gaudy, intended for vain display."

MAKE IT STICK:

Using the word *ostentatious*, describe a boastful act by someone you know or a fictitious character.

_____

_____

_____

_____

_____

_____

_____

_____

LATENT

(LAY-tunt), adjective

Existing and having the power to become visible or manifest but, for the time being, remaining unseen or unknown.

EXAMPLE:

The virus remained **LATENT** in his system for some time, causing him to unknowingly infect those with whom he came into close contact.

TRIVIA:

This word was used to describe Kris Kringle in *Miracle on 34th Street* after Macy's psychologist received a thump on his head for being difficult and dishonest: "I told you he had latent maniacal tendencies!"

MAKE IT STICK:

Using the word *latent*, describe something that is hidden but exists (from fingerprints to a lack of skills to hidden personality traits).

_____

_____

_____

_____

_____

_____

MALADY
(MAL-uh-dee), noun

A disorder or disease; an illness or unwholesome condition.

Jason's **MALADY**, had it gone undiagnosed, could have taken his life.

TRIVIA:

As the definition of the word suggests, a malady can be an illness (the term coming from Anglo-French *malade* meaning "sickness, illness, disease"), but it has also taken on a meaning of something unwholesome or negative in one's life, like a bad habit.

MAKE IT STICK:

Using *malady*, describe a situation in which a fictitious character travels to a foreign country in which he/she doesn't speak the language and is subjected to a malady.

DISCOMBOBULATE
(diss-kum-BOB-yoo-late), verb

To confuse or place into an awkward predicament; utterly disconcerted.

EXAMPLE:

The frenzied pace of eight hours on the trading floor has left me utterly **DISCOMBOBULATED**.

TRIVIA:

Despite what Milwaukee's Mitchell International Airport might have you believe with its "Recombobulation Area" for travelers, there is no positive form of *discombobulate*. You cannot combobulate or recombobulate.

MAKE IT STICK:

Using *discombobulate* as a verb, describe a humorous situation in which you were mentally or physically flustered.

PROGNATHOUS
(prog-NAY-thuss), adjective

Having a forward-thrusting jaw.

EXAMPLE:

When speaking in public, Benito Mussolini thrust his **PROGNATHOUS** jaw in the air, drew in his stomach, and put his hands on his hips.

TRIVIA:

Jaw protrusion was first deemed an important physical characteristic by the English anthropologist Sir Edward Evan Evans-Pritchard (whose name sounds like something out of an Agatha Christie novel). Correspondingly, a receding jawline is called *orthognathism*.

MAKE IT STICK:

Write a scene in which your character either has or has assumed a *prognathous* appearance.

ABSCOND
(ab-SKOND), verb

To depart quickly and in secret, especially to avoid criminal charges.

EXAMPLE:

The bank robbers immediately **ABSCONDED** to Mexico with the money.

TRIVIA:

First used in 1652, the term generally refers to any act of running away and/or hiding yourself and/or money from the law. In legal proceedings, you can abscond from trial and parole, as well as abscond with monetary funds.

MAKE IT STICK:

List three people you've read about who have recently *absconded* with money or from accountability in a crime.

1._____

2._____

3._____

HAGGIS
(HAG-iss), noun

A dish originating in Scotland made by removing the heart, liver, and lungs of a sheep or cow, dicing them, adding onions, suet, oatmeal, and seasonings, placing the mixture into the animal's stomach, and boiling it.

EXAMPLE:

Ivan had been enjoying the **HAGGIS** Mrs. MacIntyre had prepared for him until he asked her how it was made.

TRIVIA:

Common throughout England and Scotland, haggis is considered a "pudding," and the word dates from the late thirteenth century. Today's ingredients for haggis are a little more upscale and less about the entrails.

MAKE IT STICK:

You're in a Scottish pub and the owner wants to give you a complimentary serving of *haggis*. Describe the dish and how you respond.

_____
_____
_____
_____
_____
_____

GIBE
(JIBE), noun, verb

An insult; to sneer, heckle, or insult.

EXAMPLE:

We like to invite Roger to our cocktail parties as he is able to keep other guests entertained for hours on end with his stories and **GIBES**.

TRIVIA:

The homonym *jibe* is sometimes used to mean "teasing" but has the additional meaning of "to be in accord." It's often used in sailing ("Jibe the mainsail!"). Use *gibe* when you are casting insults, and use *jibe* when things are compatible.

MAKE IT STICK:

Finish this scene using *gibe* in one of your sentences: Before Ralph knew what was happening, the reporter asked what he thought of the coronation...

BÊTE NOIRE
(BET NWAHR), noun

An opponent motivated by revenge; a person's **nemesis**; one who will stop at nothing to settle a score.

EXAMPLE:

Things looked bleak; Harold's **BÊTE NOIRE**, Mike, was in charge of all hiring decisions.

TRIVIA:

As should be obvious, the term is French in origin and was first used in 1805. It literally translates as "black beast."

MAKE IT STICK:

Incorporating the term *bête noire*, write about your high school nemesis.

_____

_____

_____

_____

_____

_____

_____

_____

_____

_____

_____

_____

_____

ANTAGONIST
(an-TAG-uh-nist), noun

The bad guy in a story, novel, film, etc. The character who opposes a story's main character.

EXAMPLE:

As an **ANTAGONIST**, you can't get any better than John Milton's version of Satan in *Paradise Lost*.

TRIVIA:

Some of the most famous film antagonists include Darth Vader (Star Wars), Jack Torrance (*The Shining*), Lord Voldemort (Harry Potter), Hannibal Lecter (*The Silence of the Lambs*), Hans Gruber (*Die Hard*), and the Wicked Witch of the West (*The Wizard of Oz*).

MAKE IT STICK:

List ten *antagonists* from your favorite books.

1. _____

2. _____

3. _____

4. _____

5. _____

6. _____

7. _____

8. _____

9. _____

10. _____

GRATIS
(GRAT-iss), adjective, adverb

Free of charge.

EXAMPLE:

I liked visiting Renee when she was working at the ice cream parlor, but the **GRATIS** sundaes and banana splits she always offered were impossible to resist—and they didn't help my diet.

TRIVIA:

First used in the fifteenth century, *gratis* comes from the Latin word meaning "favor." *Gratis* can be used as both adjective and adverb. *Dessert was gratis. Dessert was served gratis.*

MAKE IT STICK:

Write a sentence using *gratis* as an adjective.

STAGNATION
(stag-NAY-shun), noun

A state of not flowing or moving.

EXAMPLE:

The river, choked with pollutants, is in a state of **STAGNATION**.

TRIVIA:

In the 1970s, the combination of soaring inflation and sluggish to nonexistent economic growth impelled economists to combine *stagnation* with *inflation* to characterize the US economy as in a state of stagflation.

MAKE IT STICK:

Describe a time, using *stagnation,* when you or a loved one seemed to be in the doldrums.

EFFLUENT
(EF-loo-unt), noun

In general, something that flows out;
more specifically, a fluid discharged as waste.

TRIVIA:

From the Latin verb *effluentem*, meaning "flowing out," the noun form first appeared in 1859. While the word does refer to other flowing sources (such as an underground spring feeding a pond or lake), its most popular use originated in the 1930s and specifically refers to sewage or other waste and pollutants pumped into the air or dumped into water.

MAKE IT STICK:

Using the words *effluent*, *attorney*, *brother-in-law*, and *unintentional*, write a court scene in which a company is testifying about its manufacturing practices.

ABET
(uh-BET), verb

To encourage or assist a plan or activity;
to entice or help, usually in a misdeed.

EXAMPLE:

Though Michael did not participate in the actual kidnapping, he left himself open to charges of **ABETTING** the perpetrators by hiding them from the police.

TRIVIA:

It was in 1790 that the newly formed United States added a statute dealing with those who perhaps didn't commit a crime themselves but aided, assisted, counseled, or advised on matters of murder or theft committed on land or at sea as well as piracy on the high seas. Abetting was broadened in 1870 to include any felony, not just murder or theft.

MAKE IT STICK:

Using the word *abet*, write a fictitious newspaper article detailing a character who abets a bank robbery.

WAGGISH
(WAG-ish), adjective

Joking, witty, and mischievous.

EXAMPLE:

Kent's **WAGGISH** comments got him in trouble with the boss.

TRIVIA:

The noun form is *wag*. Charles Lamb, in describing the upcoming summer, comments, "Summer, as my friend Coleridge waggishly writes, has set in with its usual severity."

MAKE IT STICK:

Write a short scene using the following words: *waggish, Dave, pool,* and *biker chick.*

ENMITY
(EN-mih-tee), noun

Intense hostility toward a person or thing, usually taking the form of action; a bitter dislike directed at something or someone.

EXAMPLE:

Clyde's first few months on the job were fine but, after he was transferred to a new department, he came to harbor real **ENMITY** toward his supervisor.

TRIVIA:

Enmity derives from an Anglo-French word meaning "enemy." After the Battle of Hastings in 1066, a large number of French words accompanied the Norman soldiers who invaded England. The result was a fusion of Anglo-Saxon and Old French that eventually evolved into Middle English.

MAKE IT STICK:

Using the word *enmity*, describe a situation in which you felt animosity or hostility toward a situation or individual.

GENTRIFY

(JENN-truh-fie), verb

To take something run-down, such as a neighborhood, and improve it.

EXAMPLE:

Attempts to **GENTRIFY** the historic neighborhood failed because of community apathy.

TRIVIA:

The noun form is *gentrification*. Gentrification is a controversial topic in politics and urban planning. Plans to improve neighborhoods in cities often displace people from their homes.

MAKE IT STICK:

Describe an example of *gentrification* in your city, town, or community.

FUGACIOUS

(few-GAY-shus), adjective

Existing only temporarily; brief; fleeting; transitory.

EXAMPLE:

With seven children to care for, my wife and I knew that tranquility in the house was a **FUGACIOUS** thing.

TRIVIA:

Things that are fugacious are fleeing; the word derives from the Latin *fugere*, meaning "to flee." It was first used in the seventeenth century.

MAKE IT STICK:

Using the word *fugacious*, talk about something in your life that is fleeting or never sticks around for very long.

FRIVOLITY

(frih-VOL-ih-tee), noun

The state of being unworthy of serious note or insubstantial;
a lighthearted or ludicrous act.

EXAMPLE:

We have no time for
FRIVOLITY; the manager is
coming tomorrow morning.

TRIVIA:

Michelangelo, lamenting how his art became an idol to him, said, "The world's frivolities have robbed me of the time that I was given for reflecting upon God." It's not clear if he lumped the Sistine Chapel into that category.

MAKE IT STICK:

Write a short scene incorporating *frivolity*, *Lori*, *beach ball*, and *sand*.

IMBIBE
(im-BIBE), verb

To drink; generally used to describe the drinking of alcoholic beverages; to take in (an idea).

EXAMPLE:

Donald once had a drinking problem, so now he no longer **IMBIBES**.

TRIVIA:

The first use of *imbibe* was in the fourteenth century in its meaning "to take in/drink in/soak in." While most people now use it to refer to drinking (whether an alcoholic beverage or something else), the "soak in" definition still persists. For instance, Mahatma Gandhi said, "My religion enables me, obliges me, to imbibe all that is good in all the great religions of the earth."

MAKE IT STICK:

Finish the scene incorporating the word *imbibe*: The streets were deserted. Mark looked around for his brother, whom he thought had been right next to him...

VIVACIOUS

(vy-VAY-shuss), adjective

Spirited; full of life.

EXAMPLE:

The novelist's characters are saucy and **VIVACIOUS** but the situations they face are, alas, deadly dull.

TRIVIA:

Vivacious dates back to the 1640s and comes from the Latin *vivax*, meaning "lively and vigorous" but with more of a sense of playfulness.

MAKE IT STICK:

Finish the scene incorporating *vivacious*: Kurt held out his hand. Sonja placed her hand in his and they walked to the dance floor...

CLAIRVOYANCE

(klare-VOY-uhnce), noun

Supernatural perceptive skills; the ability to perceive things normally out of the range of human senses.

EXAMPLE:

Michael claimed to have **CLAIRVOYANCE** and even held a few playful séances, but no one took his claims seriously.

TRIVIA:

From the French for "clear sight." A "sixth sense" about an outcome is an example of clairvoyance, like predicting who will win the World Series.

MAKE IT STICK:

Have you ever had or read about a *clairvoyant* experience? Describe it using today's word.

EMASCULATE

(ee-MASS-kyoo-late), verb

To castrate; to deprive of strength or essential elements.

EXAMPLE:

In the editor's view, my book had been subjected to a "deft pruning of occasional offensive passages"; in mine, it had been utterly **EMASCULATED.**

TRIVIA:

Kevin Bacon referred to being an actor as "emasculating...[people] putting makeup on you and telling you when to wake up and when to go to sleep, holding your hand to cross the street."

MAKE IT STICK:

Using the words *emasculate*, *lemonade*, *hairbrush*, and *soufflé*, describe a scene in which your character is deprived of strength or dignity.

FOOFARAW

(FOO-fuh-raw), noun

A lot of fuss about nothing;
an excessive amount of decoration
on oneself, in a room, etc.

EXAMPLE:

Whether or not the celebrity had removed
a mole became a **FOOFARAW** debated
for days by the entertainment press.

TRIVIA:

Probably from the Spanish *fanfarrón*,
meaning "boaster." Used in the American
West, its first documented use was 1848.

MAKE IT STICK:

Use *foofaraw* in two different sentences—
first as fussing about nothing and then
as excessive decoration.

1. _____
_____
_____

2. _____
_____
_____

COGNOMEN

(kog-NO-muhn), noun

A nickname.

EXAMPLE:

He doesn't mind being called "Leopold,"
but he prefers his **COGNOMEN**, "Lee."

TRIVIA:

The first known use of *cognomen* was in
1691, but the practice of distinguishing
family members by different nicknames
is steeped in family histories. This practice is particularly helpful in reducing
confusion with regard to whom one is
referencing, especially if a family has
four or five generations of Theodores!

MAKE IT STICK:

List five friends or family members who
go by a nickname, or *cognomen*.

1. _____

2. _____

3. _____

4. _____

5. _____

EXISTENTIAL

(eggs-ih-STENCH-uhl), adjective

Relating to or affirming existence;
grounded in the philosophy characterized by a belief
that individuals make their own choices and find their own
meaning of life while shunning faith in a higher being.

EXAMPLE:

While enduring another horrible day at her boring office job, Phyllis had an **EXISTENTIAL** moment and decided—right then and there— to quit and move to a new town.

TRIVIA:

The term dates back to 1937 in the philosophy and works of Søren Kierkegaard and later popularized in the writings of Jean-Paul Sartre, Simone de Beauvoir, and Albert Camus.

MAKE IT STICK:

Using the word *existential,* describe one thing that would
cause you to question the very foundation of how you've lived your life.

FROUFROU
(FROO-froo), noun

Excessive or unnecessary decoration; especially,
an elaborate adornment in women's fashion.

EXAMPLE:

Angela had never seen so many
ill-fitting tuxedoes and self-conscious
frills and **FROUFROUS** as she
beheld the night of the senior prom.

TRIVIA:

Froufrou comes from the 1870 poem
"Ma Bohème" and is a French onomatopoeia for the noise made by
skirts when women dance. Frou-Frou
is also the name of the expensive
horse Count Vronsky purchases in
Tolstoy's *Anna Karenina*. It may have
been excessive, all things considered.

MAKE IT STICK:

Describe a debutante ball, specifically adding elements
of excessive decoration and using the word *froufrou*.

JOCULAR
(JAH-kew-luhr), adjective

Wryly amusing;
strikingly odd and humorous.

EXAMPLE:

The little book was filled with **JOCULAR** illustrations that further undermined any attempt at authoritativeness.

TRIVIA:

First used in the seventeenth century, it has the same root, the Latin *jocularis*, as words such as *joke* and *jocose*. Today, being jocular is considered a positive attribute—it's not just about making jokes but being fun to be around.

MAKE IT STICK:

Describe something *jocular* you've seen recently.

FACTITIOUS
(fack-TISH-us), adjective

Lacking spontaneity; artificial; contrived.

EXAMPLE:

The news network's **FACTITIOUS** commentary seemed to be mere talking points from the current presidential administration.

TRIVIA:

First used in English in the 1640s, *factitious* derives from the Latin *factīcius*, meaning "artificial."

MAKE IT STICK:

Write a scene incorporating the word *factitious*, using it in either a literal or figurative way.

AFICIONADO
(uh-FISH-ee-uh-NAH-doe), noun

A devotee; someone enthralled with and who supports a particular activity.

My dad can't get enough of it, but I've never really been a baseball **AFICIONADO.**

Using *aficionado* in a sentence, describe someone enthralled with the Cleveland Browns.

TRIVIA:

Ernest Hemingway introduced this word of Spanish origin with his bullfighting-obsessed character Jake Barnes in the 1926 novel *The Sun Also Rises*. Hemingway himself said, "The aficionado, or lover of the bullfight, may be said, broadly, then, to be one who has this sense of the tragedy and ritual of the fight so that the minor aspects are not important except as they relate to the whole." Passion for the entirety of something, indeed.

VERVE

(vurv), noun

A spirited and enthusiastic manner, particularly when embodied in an artistic performance; an air of vitality.

EXAMPLE:

The critics were unanimous in their opinion that, although the plot of the play was implausible and its production values poor, the actress playing the librarian brought a unique **VERVE** to the show.

TRIVIA:

Originally meaning having a "special talent in writing," *verve* morphed to include meaning "mental vigor" by 1803.

MAKE IT STICK:

Finish this scene incorporating the word *verve*: Miss Georgia, though 101 years old, rested her hand on the ballet barre. "Now, girls. I'm seeing a lot of slouching. Let's try this again!"

SUFFRAGE
(SUFF-rudge), noun

The right to vote.

EXAMPLE:

Today's apathetic voters (or more precisely, nonvoters) seem to have little appreciation for how hard previous generations had to fight for the principle of universal **SUFFRAGE**.

TRIVIA:

In a skit from the sketch comedy series *The Man Show*, hosts Jimmy Kimmel and Adam Carolla ask passersby to sign a petition to end women's suffrage. Judging by the number of people who signed the petition, including women, there are many who don't understand the meaning of the word. Let's get this right, people!

MAKE IT STICK:

Write a scene from the early 1900s when women were fighting for the right to vote. Be sure to incorporate the word *suffrage*.

NEBULOUS
(NEB-yuh-luss), adjective

Cloudy; vague.

EXAMPLE:

Every time Claudia tried to ask Philip about his intentions or the future of their relationship, he gave a **NEBULOUS** reply and changed the subject.

TRIVIA:

The word derives from the Latin *nebulosus*, meaning "misty, cloudy, foggy, or full of vapor."

MAKE IT STICK:

Write a scene using the following: *nebulous, police officer, speed limit,* and *red light*.

WHIPPET
(WIP-it), noun

A short-haired, fast-running dog, similar to a greyhound.

EXAMPLE:

Like **WHIPPETS** straining before a race, the swimmers tensed at the edge of the pool, toes curled over the smooth stone of the starting line.

TRIVIA:

This speedy English dog has been around for about 400 years. Prior to that, *whippet* referred to "a brisk, nimble woman."

MAKE IT STICK:

Finish this scene using the word *whippet*: Vince tried to catch the dog as it tore by...

INCORRIGIBLE

(in-KORE-ij-uh-bul), adjective

(Apparently) incapable of being reformed; often used in a light-hearted, ironic sense.

EXAMPLE:

Young Pete was an **INCORRIGIBLE** boy, forever getting into scrapes and causing mischief.

TRIVIA:

As the von Trapp children introduce themselves to Fräulein Maria in the film *The Sound of Music*, Kurt declares, "I'm Kurt. I'm eleven. I'm incorrigible."

MAKE IT STICK:

List three characters from your favorite childhood stories who were *incorrigible*.

1. _____

2. _____

3. _____

JOSTLE

(JOS-l), verb

To bump or disrupt by means of incidental contact; to make one's way by elbowing or pushing (as through a crowd).

EXAMPLE:

Mark **JOSTLED** through the crowd but couldn't find Sharon.

TRIVIA:

Though it's been around since the 1540s, *jostle* is often used today in stock car racing lingo as cars jostle or jockey for position and bump others out of their way. It can also refer to what happens in malls during holiday season.

MAKE IT STICK:

You're waiting in line on Black Friday to buy a new TV. Describe the scene, incorporating the word *jostle*.

_____

_____

_____

_____

_____

_____

_____

_____

SEMANTICS

(suh-MAN-tics), noun

The study of meanings; the meaning or relationship of meanings of symbols and words.

EXAMPLE:

Whether we identify them as "streetwalkers" or "prostitutes," Mr. Mayor, is a matter of **SEMANTICS.**

TRIVIA:

Michel Bréal coined the term *sémantique* to describe the psychology or study of the meaning of language in 1883, and *semantics* began to crop up in English less than ten years later.

MAKE IT STICK:

Write a dialogue between a man and a woman who appear to be saying the same thing but, in reality, are not. Use *semantics* in the dialogue.

ZEALOT
(ZEL-ut), noun

A fervent or fanatical partisan (in favor of a certain cause);
a person who shows great zeal.

EXAMPLE:

Although he didn't mind overlooking an occasional error in procedure, Mr. Fallow was a **ZEALOT** when it came to posting correct numbers for an accounting period.

TRIVIA:

Coined in the early fourteenth century and meaning "member of a militant first-century Jewish sect that fiercely resisted the Romans in Palestine," the word extended to mean "fanatical enthusiast" by the 1630s.

MAKE IT STICK:

Using the word *zealot,* write a paragraph about a person who shows great zeal for reviving ice bucket challenges.

PERSPICUITY

(PER-spih-KEW-ih-tee), noun

Great clarity and precision.

EXAMPLE:

Roger's **PERSPICUITY** was so obvious to the crowd that they listened attentively to his speech.

TRIVIA:

From the Latin *perspicere*, meaning "to see through clearly," this word first appeared in the 1470s. The word *perspicacious* essentially means "one who has the capacity of perspicuity."

MAKE IT STICK:

Using the word *perspicuity*, write about the most impressive speech to which you've ever listened.

_____

_____

_____

_____

_____

_____

_____

_____

_____

SKITTISH

(SKIT-ish), adjective

Nervous and lacking confidence; uneasy about approaching a task.

EXAMPLE:

Lisa is still a bit **SKITTISH** about the computer; perhaps she can find someone to give her a hand.

TRIVIA:

First recorded around 1500 and pertaining to horses, *skittish* meant "very lively, frivolous." *Skittish* also refers to being figuratively flighty in thought.

MAKE IT STICK:

Write one or two sentences incorporating the words *skittish, cat, thunder,* and *bowl of cereal.*

_____

_____

_____

_____

_____

_____

_____

_____

_____

ENTOURAGE
(ON-too-rahj), noun

A group of associates; people who commonly surround, protect, and attend to someone of importance.

Melanie had hoped to score a front-page story by interviewing the reclusive movie star, but she never made it past his **ENTOURAGE**.

TRIVIA:

The word comes from the sixteenth century Middle French *entourer*, "to surround." By the 1800s, it meant "persons with whom one moves." Royalty and privileged people enjoy entourages, but so do bands like the Grateful Dead. Actor John Cusack played a character in *America's Sweethearts* who had a slightly different take on it: "I'm a paranoid schizophrenic. I *am* my own entourage!"

Describe a scene where a famous businesswoman enters a restaurant surrounded by her *entourage*.

TALISMAN
(TAL-iss-mun), noun

A lucky charm; an engraved object believed to possess occult powers.

EXAMPLE:

Justin was all set for the big game until he reached into his pocket and found that his **TALISMAN**—a small piece of stone from the shores of Ireland given to him by his mother—was missing.

TRIVIA:

The term has been around since the 1630s, originally meaning "magical figure cut or engraved under certain observances" and now meaning "a charm believed to ward off evil spirits," like a rabbit's foot or necklace of garlic. But, as John Quincy Adams once noted, perhaps other intangible qualities can act as a talisman: "Courage and perseverance have a magical talisman, before which difficulties disappear and obstacles vanish into thin air."

MAKE IT STICK:

Write a scene incorporating the following: *talisman, Marsha, Ron, Florida,* and *fruit salad.*

PUNCTILIOUS
(punk-TILL-ee-uss), adjective

Overly attentive to trifling details; taking great care to dispose of seemingly small matters in a formally correct way.

MAKE IT STICK:

Finish this scene using *punctilious*:
Kathi just wanted to have a simple picnic, but her sister had other ideas...

IOTA

(eye-O-tuh), noun

A minute quantity; an extremely small amount.

EXAMPLE:

Simon realized after combing through the report that there was not one **IOTA** of scientific evidence to the researcher's claim.

TRIVIA:

First seen in the English language in 1542, the expression "not one iota" comes from the Bible (Matthew 5:18): "For truly, I say to you, until heaven and earth pass away, not an *iota*, not a dot, will pass from the Law until all is accomplished."

MAKE IT STICK:

Write a scene using *iota, claim,* and *refute.*

APOGEE
(AP-o-jee), noun

The highest point; summit.

EXAMPLE:

Although his many fans might consider winning the Pulitzer to be the **APOGEE** of Marvin's writing career, in his mind, nothing would ever match the thrill of seeing his first novel in print.

TRIVIA:

Apogee was originally an astronomical term, referring to the farthest distance between the Earth or another heavenly body and an object orbiting it. From there it developed its meaning as the highest point or extension of something, often a career.

MAKE IT STICK:

Using *apogee* in one of your sentences, describe either an exciting hike or the work of an accomplished artist whom you respect.

_____

_____

_____

_____

_____

_____

_____

HORNSWOGGLE
(HORN-swah-guhl), verb

To deceive; trick.

EXAMPLE:

Fred was **HORNSWOGGLED** out of $15,000 by a con artist who convinced him to invest in nonexistent real estate.

TRIVIA:

Although the origin is unknown, some say it comes from the way a lassoed cow moves its head back and forth. Whatever the case, it seems to have originated in nineteenth-century America.

MAKE IT STICK:

Using today's word, describe a time when you were *hornswoggled*.

_____

_____

_____

_____

_____

_____

_____

_____

_____

EPHEMERAL
(ih-FEMM-uh-rul), adjective

Lasting only a short while.

EXAMPLE:

Our school's joy at winning the state basketball championship turned out to be **EPHEMERAL**, as the title was suspended when officials learned of an ineligible player on the team's roster.

TRIVIA:

Dame Maggie Smith once commented that she likes the fleeting quality of theater as opposed to movies or TV. "I like the ephemeral thing about theatre, every performance is like a ghost—it's there and then it's gone."

MAKE IT STICK:

Using the words *ephemeral*, *joy*, *commencement*, and *avenue*, describe a fleeting moment.

_____

_____

_____

_____

_____

_____

_____

_____

CYGNET
(SIG-nit), noun

A young swan.

EXAMPLE:

The proud mother swan led her brood of **CYGNETS** toward the north end of the pond.

TRIVIA:

The most famous cygnet is Hans Christian Andersen's *The Ugly Duckling*, a story that's been in publication since 1843. The word has often been associated with the quality of being small. For instance, in Cygnet, Ohio, a village in Wood County, the total population as of 2010 was 597. Now that's small!

MAKE IT STICK:

Describe a scene involving *cygnets* and two adult swans.

_____

_____

_____

_____

_____

_____

_____

_____

_____

LOLLAPALOOZA
(LA-luh-puh-LOO-zuh), noun

Something outstanding or unusual.

EXAMPLE:

The charity carnival concluded with a **LOLLAPALOOZA** of a parade in which the mayor rode a unicycle and juggled grapefruits to the sound of wild applause.

TRIVIA:

Variant spellings of *lollapalooza* include *lallapalooza* and *lalapaloozer*. The word can mean "something exceptional" (like a good book!) or "humdinger or doozy," probably from its occasional use in gambling. The gambling usage means you've tricked a player with a fake or made-up hand of cards, and it was a real lollapalooza or humdinger of a hand. Lollapalooza is also the name of a rock music festival, begun in 1991 by Jane's Addiction band member Perry Farrell, and is held (mostly annually) in Chicago's Grant Park.

MAKE IT STICK:

Describe a time you saw something that qualified as a real *lollapalooza* of a show.

_____

_____

_____

_____

_____

_____

_____

_____

_____

_____

_____

_____

_____

_____

_____

_____

_____

_____

_____

_____

_____

_____

_____

AMPHIBOLOGY

(am-fib-AH-loh-jee), noun

A statement in which one or more of the words may be interpreted in several ways, resulting in ambiguity; an expression that can be taken two ways, one of which often has sexual or threatening undertones.

EXAMPLE:

Although Japanese adult comic books must abide by some very stringent codes forbidding profanity and the overt depiction of sexual activity, they often feature a barrage of steamy **AMPHIBOLOGIES**.

TRIVIA:

Humor is steeped in amphibologies and hidden meanings. It comes from the Latin words *amphiboles* and *ballein*, meaning "hitting at both ends." Its earliest use was in the fourteenth century. Many feel amphibologies are one of the lowest forms of humor, but that didn't bother Shakespeare. His plays are filled with them!

MAKE IT STICK:

Write three different sentences that each have multiple meanings.

1. _____

_____

_____

2. _____

_____

_____

3. _____

_____

_____

ENUNCIATE

(ee-NUN-see-ate), verb

To articulate or pronounce;
to set something forth systematically and lucidly.

EXAMPLE:

The ideas he **ENUNCIATED** were simple, implementable, and accepted by all.

TRIVIA:

Great examples of those with poor enunciation often come from the music world, including Darius Rucker of Hootie & the Blowfish, Ariana Grande, and Sia. If it weren't for Lyrics.com, we'd never know what they were saying.

MAKE IT STICK:

Write a short scene using *enunciate,*
"she sells seashells by the seashore," open mic, and *Deb.*

MONIKER
(MON-ih-kur), noun

Name; nickname.

EXAMPLE:

Rock star Sting has revealed in interviews that even his parents and children refer to him by his famous **MONIKER**.

TRIVIA:

First used in the 1850s, many famous athletes, musicians, and actors have used monikers, including Little Richard, Lady Gaga, Madonna, Cher, Bono, Charo, Enya, Twiggy, Liberace, Big Papi, Mookie Wilson, and Shakira. And don't forget Schmoopie—the love-interest nickname made famous on *Seinfeld*.

MAKE IT STICK:

What are your five favorite *monikers* for your childhood friends?

1. _____

2. _____

3. _____

4. _____

5. _____

SNIT
(snit), noun

An angry or nasty mood; an irritated state.

EXAMPLE:

After his roommate spilled grape juice all over his favorite coat, Jay was in a **SNIT** for weeks.

TRIVIA:

First appearing in print in Clare Boothe Luce's 1937 play *Kiss the Boys Goodbye* and its 1941 film adaptation, a *snit* originally meant a "fit of childish temper." Molly Ivins, American newspaper columnist, author, political commentator, and humorist, said, "Listen to the people who are talking about how to fix what's wrong, not the ones who just work people into a snit over the problems."

MAKE IT STICK:

Write a few sentences about a time a friend or coworker was in a *snit*.

_____

_____

_____

_____

_____

_____

_____

OSCILLATE
(AH-si-late), verb

To swing back and forth between two points.

EXAMPLE:

Eddie's views **OSCILLATED** between conservatism and liberalism, much to the annoyance of many of his friends.

TRIVIA:

First used in the eighteenth century, the verb comes from the Latin *oscillare*, meaning "to swing."

MAKE IT STICK:

Roberto lifted the box, certain it contained an anvil. "Can you just put it over by the garage, sonny?" the old lady asked, pointing to the farthest point on her property. Finish this scene incorporating the word *oscillate*.

BREVITY
(BREV-ih-tee), noun

Shortness of duration; a terse and to the point expression.

EXAMPLE:

Thomas Paine's argument was stated with such **BREVITY** and passion that, within one short month of its publication, it seemed every colonist was in favor of independence from Britain.

TRIVIA:

Shakespeare wrote in *Hamlet*, "Since brevity is the soul of wit...I will be brief." (Some scholars believe the word was in use prior to this and Shakespeare merely made it popular.) It's a good reminder that laudable speeches are short, and good humor (or wit) is also best when brief and not overdone.

MAKE IT STICK:

Describe a recent event in detail. Next, incorporating the word *brevity*, recount the same event, but make your narrative shorter.

_____

_____

_____

_____

_____

_____

_____

_____

_____

_____

_____

_____

_____

JEJUNE

(ji-JOON), adjective

Dull or lackluster; immature or lacking in insight.

EXAMPLE:

Ralph's **JEJUNE** fantasies of stardom brought only laughs of derision from his friends.

TRIVIA:

First used in English in the 1610s, *jejune* is from the Latin *jejunus*, "empty, dry, barren," and also literally "fasting, hungry." A jejune comment or essay is figuratively barren, or empty.

MAKE IT STICK:

Write a short scene using the words *jejune, creepy, sun,* and *Los Angeles.*

PALINDROME
(PAL-in-drome), noun

A word or sentence that reads the same forward and backward (such as "racecar" or "Not so, Boston").

EXAMPLE:

James's dogged attempt to write a novel consisting solely of a single sixty-word **PALINDROME** led his relatives to wonder whether his best days as a writer were behind him.

TRIVIA:

Words, sentences, and dates can be palindromes. The longest palindromic word in the *Oxford English Dictionary* is *tattarrattat*, coined in James Joyce's *Ulysses* and meaning "a knock on the door." The most recent palindromic date was 02/02/2020, and most of us won't be around for the next one on 12/12/2121.

MAKE IT STICK:

Write two sentences: the first incorporates the word *palindrome* and the second IS a palindrome. (They can be brief!)

1. _____

_____

2. _____

_____

COITUS
(KO-uh-tus), noun

Sexual intercourse.

EXAMPLE:

Professor Wells sternly informed me that he prefers I use the term **COITUS** in describing the activities of the test couples rather than the less formal "making whoopee."

TRIVIA:

Dating back to 1845, it became more well known in recent years as Sheldon Cooper's term of choice in describing intercourse on the hit TV show *The Big Bang Theory*. Writers probably chose the word because it sounds more intellectual than other terms describing the same activity.

MAKE IT STICK:

You're sitting in a bar. What are the three worst pickup lines you could hear from an unsavory barfly hoping to get lucky and have coitus with you tonight? Be sure at least one of them uses the word *coitus*!

1. _____

2. _____

3. _____

BATHOS
(BATH-oss), noun

Something excessively trivial, sentimental, or melodramatic; a ludicrous change from the high-minded to the commonplace.

EXAMPLE:

The play's **BATHOS** made it hard for me to take it seriously, but June thought it was the most moving drama she'd ever seen.

TRIVIA:

With its origins from the Greek *báthos*, meaning "depth," eighteenth-century English poet Alexander Pope gave *bathos* its current meaning, in which something makes "a descent from the sublime to the ridiculous." Someone's lofty goals or a novel's ambitious plot can make a downturn into something melodramatic or overly sentimental.

MAKE IT STICK:

List three examples from novels, plays, or films that exemplify *bathos*.

1. _____

2. _____

3. _____

CACOPHONOUS
(ka-KOFF-a-nuss), adjective

Loud, discordant; clashing.

EXAMPLE:

Pop music has always struck some adults as **CACOPHONUS**.

TRIVIA:

First arising in the late 1700s, the word derives from the Greek *kakos*, meaning "bad" or "evil" and *phone*, meaning "voice." The word applies to a good deal of modern music, both pop and classical—the compositions of Philip Glass, for instance.

MAKE IT STICK:

Using the word *cacophonous*, describe a room decorated in a series of clashing styles.

_____
_____
_____
_____
_____
_____
_____
_____
_____
_____
_____
_____

LATKE
(LOT-kuh), noun

A Jewish potato pancake often eaten during Hanukkah.

EXAMPLE:

Mrs. Bloom always made her famous **LATKES** for the children during the holiday season.

TRIVIA:

Latkes have been prepared with potatoes since at least the 1800s (when the potato arrived in Eastern Europe), but older versions of the pancake, made with cheeses like ricotta, date back to the Middle Ages.

MAKE IT STICK:

Describe a holiday setting using *latkes, China, Jayne,* and *leg.*

NOSH
(nahsh), verb

The process of nibbling or snacking on something.

EXAMPLE:

Before we go to the movie, let's **NOSH** on some chips.

TRIVIA:

This is a Yiddish word for "nibble or gnaw." Carol Burnett, when discussing how she keeps her slim figure, commented, "My interesting diet tips are eat early and don't nosh between meals."

MAKE IT STICK:

In a few sentences or a short paragraph, describe a time you were ravenous. What did you *nosh* on? Who was with you?

YABBER
(YAB-bur), verb

To jabber; to chatter meaninglessly.

EXAMPLE:

I am not interested in any of your **YABBERING** about how busy you've been at home; I want to know why this work is a month and a half late.

TRIVIA:

Yabber appeared in 1855 and has its roots in Gabi, an Australian Aboriginal language, and could be an alteration of *jabber*. You might feel sports commentators, your mother-in-law, or the person sitting next to you on a red-eye from Los Angeles to New York City all yabber too much if they talk endlessly about something that holds no interest for you.

MAKE IT STICK:

Write a humorous scene incorporating the words *yabber*, *train*, *rolling pin*, and *rabbit*.

JETTISON
(JET-ih-sun), verb

To cast off or overboard.
Similarly, to abandon something
once thought valuable that has
since become a burden.

EXAMPLE:

The project seemed promising initially,
but with the looming possibility they
could be accused of having a conflict
of interest, Ted and Jan decided to
JETTISON their plans.

TRIVIA:

The noun version of *jettison* has been
part of the English language since the
fifteenth century, and the verb joined
the language in the nineteenth century.

MAKE IT STICK:

List three things you could *jettison*
from your life right now and never miss:

1. _____

2. _____

3. _____

JULIENNE
(joo-lee-EN), adjective, noun

In thin strips (of vegetables); the
soup containing such **vegetables**.

EXAMPLE:

Lisa knew **JULIENNED** vegetables
would look more elegant on the plates
of her dinner guests than those cut in
the normal way.

TRIVIA:

The first known use of this French term
in print is from François Massialot's
1722 cookbook *Le Cuisinier Royal et
Bourgeois*. In English, the first use was in
the eighteenth century as a soup made
of chopped vegetables.

MAKE IT STICK:

Write out a recipe step in which you
must cut the vegetables *julienne* style.

_____
_____
_____
_____
_____
_____
_____
_____

DILLYDALLY
(DIH-lee-DAA-lee), verb

To waste time; to loiter or loaf.

"If you don't stop **DILLYDALLYING**," Mrs. Adams scolded her husband, "we'll be late for the opera."

Describe an incident in which you were in a rush but your companion dawdled. Be sure to use *dillydally*.

TRIVIA:

The term was first used in 1741. It's possible it began with the word *dally*, meaning "delay," and the *dilly* bit is possibly a corruption of *daily*. But the iconic use of the term comes from the movie classic *The Princess Bride*. Inigo Montoya says, "Let me sum up. Buttercup is marry Humperdinck in little less than half an hour. So all we have to do is get in, break up the wedding, steal the princess, make our escape...after I kill Count Rugen." Westley replies, "That doesn't leave much time for dillydallying."

NOXIOUS
(NOK-shuss), adjective

Harmful; injurious; having a corrupting or debilitating influence.

EXAMPLE:

The **NOXIOUS** weed soon took over the entire crop, which eventually failed.

TRIVIA:

The word dates back to the 1500s and comes from the Latin *noxius* ("hurtful or injurious"). While the word can still mean something harmful or even fatal, like lethal gases, it is also used in exaggeration about unpleasant experiences or smells, such as a van full of sweaty boys after a baseball game or your Aunt Clara's corned beef and cabbage.

MAKE IT STICK:

In a few sentences or a short paragraph, describe a brief scene incorporating the words *cleats*, *heat*, **noxious**, and *french fries*.

DERRING-DO
(DARE-ing-DOO), noun

Heroic deeds; acts of bravery.

EXAMPLE:

Luke Skywalker's challenges and feats of **DERRING-DO** are perhaps the most memorable elements of the original Star Wars trilogy.

TRIVIA:

Geoffrey Chaucer first used *derring-do* in passages as a verb with the meaning "daring to do" (what is proper to a brave knight).

MAKE IT STICK:

Write a short scene incorporating the following: *derring-do, puppies, truck, Marty,* and *cliff.*

BOMBAST
(BOM-bast), noun

Haughty, overblown, or pompous talk or writing; an exaggerated rhetorical style.

EXAMPLE:

We expected a compelling argument from our attorney, but he came to court offering little more than **BOMBAST**.

TRIVIA:

Bombast, in its original meaning, referred to the soft, fluffy down of the cotton plant, but it quickly morphed to mean the fluff of speech.

MAKE IT STICK:

Which modern-day public figures exhibit the most *bombast* when speaking to an audience?

NOMENCLATURE
(NO-men-klat-cher), noun

A system of names for purposes of organization; a technical, professional, or artistic set or system of names in a given discipline.

EXAMPLE:
Harold had a good grasp of the fundamental principles of chemistry, but his knowledge of the **NOMENCLATURE** of chemical compounds was weak.

TRIVIA:
From the Latin *nōmen*, meaning "name," and *calāre*, meaning "to announce, proclaim," it is the basis of order in the arts and sciences.

MAKE IT STICK:
What system of *nomenclature* are you familiar with? Plants? Animals? Music? Write a few sentences and argue for or against changing nomenclature as new information is learned.

_____
_____
_____
_____
_____
_____
_____

DIATRIBE
(DIE-uh-tribe), noun

Bitter denunciation; a pointed and abusive critique.

EXAMPLE:
The professor had scrawled a scathing **DIATRIBE** in red on the unfortunate student's paper.

TRIVIA:
While having its early roots in Latin, the modern use of *diatribe* in English came about in 1804 with the "bitter and violent criticism" use of the word. Nowadays, we need only turn to social media to see diatribes posted on every topic imaginable.

MAKE IT STICK:
What are three examples from recent books you've read or TV shows you've watched where a character delivers a *diatribe*?

1. _____
   _____

2. _____
   _____

3. _____
   _____

EXTEMPORANEOUS

(ex-tem-por-AN-e-us), adjective

Spontaneous; not planned or rehearsed; spur of the moment.

MAKE IT STICK:

Finish the scene using the word *extemporaneous*:
Beth had always hated speaking in public, and now her maid of honor was introducing her to say a few words to the wedding guests.

UNCEREMONIOUS
(UN-sare-uh-MONE-ee-uss), adjective

Rude or abrupt; tactlessly hasty; inappropriate.

EXAMPLE:

June made an **UNCEREMONIOUS** exit just as the chairman was beginning his remarks on the Fentworth project.

TRIVIA:

Many CEOs or management employees are unceremoniously removed from their positions when companies change ownership, and many high-profile radio and TV personalities can be removed quickly for a myriad of reasons. Matt Lauer, for instance, was fired from NBC's *Today* show in 2017 after allegations of inappropriate sexual behavior.

MAKE IT STICK:

Write a short scene incorporating the following:
Danielle, **unceremonious**, *roller skating rink*, and *popcorn*.

CONTUMELIOUS

(con-too-MEH-lee-uss), adjective

Rude and arrogant; insulting or disrespectful (especially speech).

EXAMPLE:

Her **CONTUMELIOUS** retorts to Joan's well-intentioned queries stunned the dinner party.

TRIVIA:

First used in the fifteenth century, it has the additional meaning of "angry and contemptuous."

MAKE IT STICK:

Write a babysitting scene involving an insolent child, using *contumelious*.

_____
_____
_____
_____
_____
_____
_____
_____
_____
_____
_____

BILDUNGSROMAN

(BILL-dungs-roh-man), noun

A coming-of-age novel or novel where a character undergoes moral and psychological growth.

EXAMPLE:

I enjoyed Professor Graham's class, but I wish he hadn't limited us to studies of **BILDUNGSROMANS**.

TRIVIA:

Some of the most famous bildungsromans are *The Catcher in the Rye*, *To Kill a Mockingbird*, *Emma*, *Jane Eyre*, *A Tree Grows in Brooklyn*, and *The Kite Runner*.

MAKE IT STICK:

List three books you feel fit the description of *bildungsromans*.

1. _____

2. _____

3. _____

ARGOT
(ARE-go), noun

Secret words and idioms used by particular groups.

EXAMPLE:

With the advent of text messaging, it has become even more difficult to follow the **ARGOT** of teenagers.

TRIVIA:

First making its appearance in the 1520s, *argot* is from Middle French, meaning "language of thieves and vagabonds."

MAKE IT STICK:

Using the words *argot*, *racetrack*, *mint julep*, and *feather*, write a scene from the Kentucky Derby, making up your own argots if necessary to reflect the dialogue and jargon of the day.

DENOUEMENT
(day-new-MAH), noun

The resolution of a plot following its climax. In general, it is the wrapping-up or outcome of any complex series of events.

EXAMPLE:

I was disappointed with the play because I felt its **DENOUEMENT** left too many loose ends.

MAKE IT STICK:

Think of a recent novel you've read that had an unsatisfying *denouement*. Write a different ending!

TRIVIA:

From the French word for "untying." While used mainly in literature, film, and theater, *denouement* can also apply to daily dealings, such as unraveling and understanding the details underlying arguments between friends. Edgar Allan Poe believed "every plot, worth the name, must be elaborated to its denouement before anything be attempted with the pen." This would certainly help avoid an unsatisfying resolution of a plot!

PROSELYTIZE
(PROSS-uh-luh-tize), verb

To attempt (often overbearingly) to convert to one's own religious faith.

EXAMPLE:

It is not my intention to **PROSELYTIZE** but rather to share some insights on my own experiences within the Jewish faith.

TRIVIA:

Originally from the 1670s, *proselytize* initially referred to religious evangelism in which you tried to persuade someone to switch to your religious beliefs or your way of living and has since expanded to include trying to convert someone to any belief, whether a political view, an exercise regime, or a juice-cleansing ritual you're convinced would benefit everyone.

MAKE IT STICK:

Using *proselytize*, write a scene in which a neighbor or friend is trying to persuade you to join them in a lifestyle choice.

BALK

(bock), verb, noun

To hesitate and refuse to go forward; to prevent from accomplishing an aim; to stop oneself in order to consider whether or not to go on. In baseball: to perform an illegal maneuver in the delivery of a throw from the pitching mound; an instance of such an illegal delivery.

EXAMPLE:

At first, Mona **BALKED** at the suggestion that she apply for the position in management; she did not like the idea of working late hours.

TRIVIA:

From the Old English *balca*, meaning "ridge, bank," the old use was for "an unplowed strip in a field, often along and marking a boundary," perhaps as something that would cause a person to come up short, pause, or hesitate. Today, we use *balk* figuratively as a hindrance, obstruction, or something that causes us to hesitate because we don't initially like the idea of it.

MAKE IT STICK:

Finish this scene using the word *balk*: John proposed golf, thinking Stacey would decline. Little did he know she shot an 87 in the last tournament...

CODGER

(KOD-jur), noun

A peculiar or eccentric man, generally of advanced years.

TRIVIA:

While the original meaning of this word when it appeared in 1756 alluded to an odd person or a miserly man, its modern interpretation is of an eccentric man who is also considered endearing. The word stems from *cadger*, an antiquated word meaning "beggar." In the movie *Grand Torino*, Clint Eastwood plays a codger living in Detroit.

MAKE IT STICK:

Tell about an old *codger* with whom you've had a fond interaction.

LUMMOX

(LUM-ox), noun

A dim-witted and awkward person; an oaf.

TRIVIA:

First used in 1825 to refer to a "clumsy, stupid man," the word might be influenced by the slang insult *dumb ox* and could also have morphed from the act of lumbering (from the verb *lummock*, meaning to "move heavily or clumsily").

MAKE IT STICK:

Write a haiku or short ditty (à la Dr. Seuss) using the word *lummox*.

UNKEMPT
(un-KEMPT), adjective

Disheveled or messy;
lacking care in aspect or look.

EXAMPLE:

The witness's story was believable, but
the defendant's lawyer worried about his
UNKEMPT appearance.

TRIVIA:

From the 1570s and the opposite of
kempt, meaning "well-combed, neat,"
you are quite literally uncombed, or your
hair is, if you are unkempt.

MAKE IT STICK:

Write one or two sentences using
the following words: *apartment,*
unkempt, and *birthday.*

ACROPHOBIA
(ak-ruh-FO-bee-a), noun

An abnormal fear of heights
characterized by feelings of dread,
danger, and helplessness.

EXAMPLE:

Of course, his **ACROPHOBIA**
ruled out a ride in the hot-air balloon.

TRIVIA:

Probably the most famous cinematic
character with crippling acrophobia was
Scottie Ferguson, played by James Stewart, in Alfred Hitchcock's 1958 thriller,
Vertigo. Between 2 and 5 percent of the
population have acrophobia, usually as a
result of some traumatic experience.

MAKE IT STICK:

Describe a comical situation
involving *acrophobia* that happens
while visiting the Empire State
Building in New York City.

DISEQUILIBRIUM
(dis-ek-wih-LIB-ree-um), noun

A sensation of dizziness and disorientation;
a feeling of tilting or spinning.

EXAMPLE:

Jane was overcome with a
sudden bout of **DISEQUILIBRIUM**
as the ship left port.

TRIVIA:

Disequilibrium sometimes goes away
on its own, without the need for
medical intervention. Why? Because
the brain adapts by shifting to other
mechanisms that allow the person to
maintain his or her balance.

MAKE IT STICK:

Write a paragraph incorporating *disequilibrium,*
barstool, Pete, Phil, and *neon sign.*

IDIOSYNCRASY

(id-ee-oh-SINK-ra-see), noun

An odd behavioral or
personality characteristic.

TRIVIA:

On the sitcom *The Big Bang Theory*,
much is made of Sheldon's idiosyncra-
sies. At one point, Sheldon says to Leon-
ard, "Years from now my biographer
might ask you about this event." Leon-
ard replies, "Oh, I have *so* many things
to tell your biographer."

MAKE IT STICK:

Describe a person or character,
either in fiction or real life, who has
odd personality characteristics.
Use the word *idiosyncrasy*.

PATOIS

(PAH-twah), noun

The specialized language or
vocabulary of a particular profession,
trade, or hobby; the particular
dialect of a region.

EXAMPLE:

The book asks the reader to make sense
of some rather sophisticated **PATOIS**
likely to be comprehensible only to those
familiar with accounting procedures.

TRIVIA:

Patois is generally regarded as a version
of a language considered nonstandard.
For instance, the dialects of English spoken in countries such as Jamaica or the
Bahamas are regarded as patois.

MAKE IT STICK:

Write a short dialogue between
two people using jargon while
incorporating the word *patois*.

ELOCUTION
(el-oh-KYOO-shun), noun

A style of public speech.

EXAMPLE:

The cast's **ELOCUTION** left a great deal to be desired.

TRIVIA:

Most famous speeches in history get their notoriety from both content and delivery. Think Martin Luther King Jr.'s "I Have a Dream," JFK's inaugural address, and Winston Churchill's "We Shall Fight on the Beaches."

MAKE IT STICK:

Describe a speech you heard in which the speaker had superb *elocution*. What made the speaker so effective?

_____
_____
_____
_____
_____
_____
_____
_____
_____
_____
_____
_____

BEFUDDLE
(bee-FUD-il), verb

To confuse or perplex; to mystify or confuse, as with bewildering arguments or misleading **statements.**

EXAMPLE:

His vague account of strange doings in the woods succeeded in **BEFUDDLING** the police officers and probably saved him a traffic ticket.

TRIVIA:

Fuddle, circa 1600, meant "to confuse with drink," and the modern-day term dates to 1873 in reference to both "to confuse with drink" as well as merely "to confuse or perplex (without drink)."

MAKE IT STICK:

List five topics you're *befuddled* by but would like to know more about. Pick one to read about this week.

1. _____

2. _____

3. _____

4. _____

5. _____

EFFERVESCENT
(eff-ur-VESS-unt), adjective

Bubbly; sparkling; lively.

EXAMPLE:

Myra's **EFFERVESCENT** personality makes her a favorite guest at our parties.

TRIVIA:

Effervescent has been in use since the 1650s and comes from the Latin *effervēscere*, meaning the "action of boiling up," more so than "bubbly." Its figurative use, for a personality that is lively and bubbly, is from 1748, but it also refers to actual bubbles, as in champagne and also Alka-Seltzer's effervescent tablets that you might need the following morning!

MAKE IT STICK:

Write a scene using the following:
effervescent, chiffon, Alison, platter, and *composer.*

ADUMBRATE

(ADD-um-brate), verb

To suggest or disclose
something partially.

EXAMPLE:

The factory workers were nervous
when they learned the owner had
ADUMBRATED a plan for layoffs.

TRIVIA:

Adumbrate is built on the Latin verb *adumbrare*, which is derived from the Latin *umbra*, meaning "shadow" or "shade." To adumbrate is to offer a shadowy view of something; the word tends to show up most often in academic or political writing.

MAKE IT STICK:

Write a short summary of a book you
recently read that hinted at or partially
suggested things to come.

FLUMMOX

(FLUHM-ucks), verb

To completely bewilder or confuse.

EXAMPLE:

No matter how much I study, mathematics continues to **FLUMMOX** me.

TRIVIA:

The origin of the word *flummox* is not quite clear, which is fitting for this word. It may have derived from the similar-sounding *lummox*, meaning "an ungainly oaf." Both words originated in 1800s English literature.

MAKE IT STICK:

Write about a topic that *flummoxes* you,
being sure to use today's word.

WAFT

(waft), verb

To carry lightly,
as if caught in a breeze.

EXAMPLE:

The scent of bread **WAFTED**
from the corner bakery.

TRIVIA:

Originally meaning "to move gently
(through the air)," *waft* is also related to
waken, meaning "rouse from sleep."

MAKE IT STICK:

Finish the scene using the word *waft*:
Tricia pulled the loaves of
French bread from the oven...

_____
_____
_____
_____
_____
_____
_____
_____
_____
_____
_____
_____
_____

LEGERDEMAIN

(lej-ur-duh-MANE), noun

Illusions performed by a magician;
sleight of hand.

EXAMPLE:

With his remarkable ability to make
everyday objects seem to disappear, the
Amazing Mannini was a true master of
LEGERDEMAIN.

TRIVIA:

Literally meaning "light of hand" and
used as an alternative to the older
"sleight (or sly) of hand," *legerdemain* is
usually used in reference to magicians
and those cheating at a game of cards.

MAKE IT STICK:

Describe a scene at a poker table in
Las Vegas incorporating *legerdemain*.

_____
_____
_____
_____
_____
_____
_____
_____
_____
_____

PEREGRINATION

(pear-uh-grih-NAY-shun), noun

Journeys or wanderings made on foot.

EXAMPLE:

Wally's Sunday **PEREGRINATIONS** took him from shuttered shops to rivers spoiled by centuries of pollution.

TRIVIA:

From twelfth-century French *peregrination*, meaning "pilgrimage, long absence," the term was first used in English in the early fifteenth century to encompass "a journey, pilgrimage."

MAKE IT STICK:

Using the words *peregrination, Ralph, Europe,* and *backpack,* describe a scene in which a journey takes place.

QUANTUM
(KWAHN-tuhm), noun

A discrete share or portion;
something that can be counted.

EXAMPLE:

Mike assumed his bridges were burned,
without assessing the **QUANTUM**
of changes he'd brought about.

TRIVIA:

From the Latin meaning "how great."
Quantum was introduced to physics
thanks to Max Planck, a German
theoretical physicist who discovered the
quantum of action in 1900, a development that led to quantum theory.

MAKE IT STICK:

Write a few sentences using *quantum*
and how yours or a character's action
resulted in an amount or reaction that
can be measured.

ANOMALOUS
(uh-NAH-muh-luss), adjective

New; unparalleled;
not having been done before.

EXAMPLE:

The studio granted Lewis **ANOMALOUS**
access to the group's session tapes
and related recording materials.

TRIVIA:

The 2016 motion picture *Sully* quotes
Chesley "Sully" Sullenberger, who
landed a disabled Airbus A320 on the
Hudson River in January 2009, as saying, "Everything is unprecedented until
it happens for the first time." Miracu-
lously, in a highly anomalous result, all
155 people on board the plane lived.

MAKE IT STICK:

Write about something new or
unparalleled you've witnessed recently,
using the word *anomalous*.

OSSIFY
(OSS-ih-fye), verb

To harden or become bonelike; literally, to change into a bone;
often used to describe a rigidity of outlook or opinion.

EXAMPLE:

The creative team's concepts, which had originally seemed very promising, had **OSSIFIED** into a conventional set of ideas.

TRIVIA:

Most of the bones of the human skeleton begin as hyaline cartilage and ossify into bony tissue. The two main forms of ossification occur in different bones: Intramembranous ossification includes bones such as the skull, and endochondral ossification includes bones such as the vertebrae.

MAKE IT STICK:

Write a short humorous scene using the words
ossify, yarn, Grandma, and *housecoat.*

INCUBUS

(IN-ku-buss), noun

A male demon believed to visit people while they slept; someone who causes stress or anxiety.

EXAMPLE:

The project was hard enough to complete without the added burden of a tyrannical boss acting as **INCUBUS** to all of the team members.

TRIVIA:

The more common definition of this word is "an evil spirit." This legendary evil ghost crushed sleepers, triggering terrible nightmares and leaving them to wake in a panic, as if they were being suffocated. In the Middle Ages they even passed laws against these ephemeral intruders. But they were difficult to prosecute.

MAKE IT STICK:

Using the word *incubus*, describe a scene in which you or a character had an impossible project assigned at the last minute.

FRUITLESSNESS
(FROOT-liss-ness), noun

That which is characterized by uselessness;
something impractical that yields nothing of value.

TRIVIA:

When you can't see the point in even trying, that's fruitlessness. Even Galileo, who valued scientific truth, backed off his morals. According to writer Albert Camus in *The Myth of Sisyphus*, "Galileo, who held a scientific truth of great importance, abjured it with the greatest ease as soon as it endangered his life. In a certain sense, he did right....To tell the truth, it is a futile question."

MAKE IT STICK:

Describe a time when your effort toward achieving something was *fruitless*.

BLATHER
(BLATH-er), verb

To gabble or talk ridiculously; talking nonsense or discussing meaningless issues for extended periods.

EXAMPLE:

We tried to leave the party but Mark insisted on **BLATHERING** endlessly to the hostess about his new car.

MAKE IT STICK:

Using the word *blather*, recount a situation in which you or a friend chattered on and on.

TRIVIA:

Dating back to the 1520s, *blather* has its Scottish roots in an Old Norse term meaning "to wag the tongue." A blatherskite or blatherskate was one who talked nonsense. The song "Maggie Lauder," featuring the term *blatherskate*, was popular among Continental Army soldiers during the American Revolution:

Who would not be in love with bonnie Maggie Lauder?
A piper met her goin' to Fife and asked what people called her.
Right scornfully she answered him, "Begone you lazy beggar!
Jog on your way, you blatherskate!
My name is Maggie Lauder."

BURLESQUE
(ber-LESK), noun

A satirically humorous imitation or mocking interpretation of a well-known work, person, or institution.

EXAMPLE:

The *Life in Hell* comic strip was an irreverent **BURLESQUE** of parents, school, and the working world.

TRIVIA:

Burlesque, derived from an Italian word meaning "mockery," is a variety show that incorporates comedy, parody, and risqué acts. In the mid-1800s, it began to include forms of striptease. Major stars such as Fanny Brice got their start in burlesque shows before going on to fame and fortune on Broadway.

MAKE IT STICK:

Write a short *burlesque* of a cooking show or golf tournament.

NEFARIOUS

(ne-FAH-ree-uss), adjective

Evil; reprehensible.

> **EXAMPLE:**
>
> Because of the **NEFARIOUS** nature of this crime, I am forced to pass a stern sentence.

> **TRIVIA:**
>
> The etymology of this is pretty straightforward: *ne*, from the Latin "not," and *fas*, from the Latin "right." Its first use was in 1609.

> **MAKE IT STICK:**
>
> What are the five most *nefarious* crimes that have happened in your lifetime?

1. _____

2. _____

3. _____

4. _____

5. _____

ONEROUS

(OWE-nur-uss), adjective

Troublesome and burdensome; entailing a heavy obligation.

> **EXAMPLE:**
>
> This contract—a thoroughly one-sided agreement—is perhaps the most **ONEROUS** document I have ever seen.

> **TRIVIA:**
>
> Actor William Shatner once said, "My kids say if there's any family dinner that doesn't result in someone crying, it's not a good dinner. They cry because it helps relieve them of a guilt or some onerous emotional burden. It's like a family tradition."

> **MAKE IT STICK:**
>
> The hunched man next door carries a horrible secret. Describe in one or two sentences, using the word *onerous*, the weight he must carry.

_____
_____
_____
_____
_____
_____
_____
_____
_____

INDOMITABLE
(in-DOM-ih-tah-bul), adjective

Courageous, bold; brave.

EXAMPLE:

I made an **INDOMITABLE** effort to complete the project by the deadline, but in the end I had to get an extension from my boss.

TRIVIA:

In the 1600s, the word meant "wild" or "untamable." Gradually, these words came to be seen as virtues, and today, to be seen as indomitable is the equivalent of courageous.

MAKE IT STICK:

Finish the scene incorporating *indomitable*:
Mary stared at the back of the delivery truck. It was full, and the driver was nowhere to be found. Sighing, she grabbed the hand truck...

RIGMAROLE

(RIG-muh-role), noun

Nonsensically complicated procedure;
misleading and incomprehensible double-talk.

EXAMPLE:

I've had enough of this author's **RIGMAROLE**; I want a book with some substance to it.

TRIVIA:

Rigmarole dates back to the thirteenth century, when King Edward I forced members of Scottish nobility to sign oaths of allegiance to him. These parchment rolls of "nonsense" came to be known as the Ragman Rolls. Over time, *Ragman Roll* became *rigmarole*.

MAKE IT STICK:

Finish the scene using *rigmarole*: Erica sat and listened as the attorney cross-examined the witness, trying to catch her in a lie.

GULLIBLE

(GULL-ih-bull), adjective

Easily cheated, tricked, or deceived.

EXAMPLE:

I'm afraid Terry is a little too **GULLIBLE** to survive for long as an aspiring actor in a city like New York.

TRIVIA:

When you're gullible, the joke is on you. One of the funniest spins on this word is from the 1953 Warner Bros. cartoon "Bully for Bugs," in which Bugs Bunny pops up in the middle of a bullfight in Mexico. He repeatedly tricks Toro the bull and at one point exclaims, "What a gulli-bull! What a nin-cow-poop!"

MAKE IT STICK:

Write a scene with two friends who are both *gullible*.

_____
_____
_____
_____
_____
_____
_____
_____
_____
_____
_____
_____
_____
_____
_____
_____

EXCULPATE
(EKS-kul-pate), verb

Proven correct or innocent despite previous indications to the contrary.

TRIVIA:

To exonerate is to clear someone of the accusation and suspicion surrounding the situation. By contrast, to be exculpated may clear you of a crime, but the suspicion remains. Lizzie Borden, O.J. Simpson, and Casey Anthony are all individuals who were exculpated, but very few people consider them exonerated.

MAKE IT STICK:

Write a short scene incorporating *lawyer*, **exculpate**, *Lisa*, and *child custody*.

FLOTSAM
(FLOT-sum), noun

The debris from a shipwreck that floats or is washed ashore.

MAKE IT STICK:

Describe a situation from the 1800s that would involve a sinking ship and *flotsam*. What is washing ashore? Who is waiting to claim it?

TRIVIA:

In maritime law, there are different types of shipwrecks with their own special laws: *flotsam, jetsam, lagan,* and *derelict.* In the case of flotsam, either the goods have been cast off by the crew as a last-ditch effort to save the vessel, or the ship has sunk and its cargo is floating on the ocean's surface. In terms of maritime law, there's no clear way of defining the ownership of goods floating in the open sea or washing up on shore, so the person who discovers flotsam is usually allowed to claim it.

HOVEL
(HUV-ul), noun

A modest, humble home or hut; a rude or dirty dwelling place.

EXAMPLE:

In the storm scenes of *King Lear*, Edgar is disguised as Poor Tom, a lunatic who has sought shelter in a **HOVEL** on the barren heath.

TRIVIA:

Though dating to the mid-fourteenth century, *hovel* as it refers to a dirty place of habitation came along in the 1620s. Often round and not built out of sturdier materials like stone or wood, hovels can be built into the sides of hills or in the ground—as J.R.R. Tolkien's hobbits did—or they can be stand-alone structures.

MAKE IT STICK:

Describe a medieval scene incorporating the word *hovel*.

SANCTIMONIOUS

(sank-tih-MONE-ee-uss), adjective

Hypocritical; two-faced, especially with
regard to matters of morals or religion.

Despite his **SANCTIMONIOUS**
braying on issues of "family values,"
Reverend Wilton certainly seems to
know his way around a certain part of
town, at least according to the reporter
who trailed him there last night.

From around 1600 and originally
meaning "measure for measure" and
"making a show of sanctity," its use
since the early 1800s is in the ironic
sense. Pretty much summed up as
holier-than-thou, a sanctimonious
hypocrite tells you to cut down your
sugar intake while enjoying a brownie
sundae with extra fudge on top.

Finish the scene using the word *sanctimonious*:
Four-year-old Megan watched as her mom removed her own half-eaten
dinner from the table and proceeded to get a bowl of ice cream.
"Can I have ice cream too?" Megan asked. "Yes. After you finish your dinner."

HUBBUB
(HUB-ub), noun

A commotion; outburst.

EXAMPLE:

The **HUBBUB** outside our window came as a surprise; the parade was not due for an hour.

TRIVIA:

Most likely of Irish origin sometime in the mid-1500s, *hubbub* may also link to the Gaelic interjection of *ub ub*, meaning "to express aversion or contempt."

MAKE IT STICK:

Using the word *hubbub,* describe a recent news event that caused a commotion.

DIMINUTIVE
(dih-MIN-you-tiv), adjective

Extremely small.

EXAMPLE:

Sometimes, trying to decipher the **DIMINUTIVE** names, numbers, and signs on a map only makes me feel more lost.

TRIVIA:

It's possible (and common) to create diminutive forms of various English words (*pig* from *piglet*, *book* from *booklet*, and *bus* from *autobus*, for example). This is also true in other languages.

MAKE IT STICK:

Write a sentence or short paragraph incorporating *elephant, diminutive,* and *jungle.*

HOBGOBLIN
(HOB-gob-lin), noun

A goblin purported to engage in mischievous behavior.

EXAMPLE:

Ever since I read her those fairy stories the other night, my daughter has tried to convince me that a **HOBGOBLIN** is responsible for every piece of mischief she gets into.

TRIVIA:

Two famous hobgoblins are Shakespeare's Puck from *A Midsummer Night's Dream* and Roderick Kingsley of Marvel's *The Amazing Spider-Man* comic book series. While some references to hobgoblins imply spirits that are fiendish in nature, today's hobgoblin is almost always engaged in some sort of mischief.

MAKE IT STICK:

Write a scene incorporating the words *hobgoblin, wrought iron, dew,* and *lantern.*

BRUMMAGEM
(BRUHM-uh-juhm), noun, adjective

Something that looks great
but performs poorly;
cheaply showy.

EXAMPLE:

I would have been better off getting an
old heap with a good engine than buying
this snazzy-looking **BRUMMAGEM**.

TRIVIA:

This word dates back to the early 1800s
and is linked to Birmingham, England,
and the town's sordid reputation for
both counterfeiting and mass-producing
consumer items of inferior quality.

MAKE IT STICK:

Describe a purchase you've made
that turned out to be a *brummagem*.

_____
_____
_____
_____
_____
_____
_____
_____
_____

ADDLE
(ADD-ull), verb, adjective

To cause something to spoil;
to make confused.

EXAMPLE:

You're going to **ADDLE** the milk if you
don't put it back in the refrigerator!

TRIVIA:

First used in the thirteenth century
to essentially mean "a rotten egg,"
it became an adjective in the 1600s,
meaning "putrid or rotten."

MAKE IT STICK:

Use *addled* in two different sentences—
one in the literal sense of "to spoil"
and the second in the figurative sense of
"to make confused."

1. _____
_____
_____

2. _____
_____
_____

JETSAM
(JET-sum), noun

Material thrown overboard to lighten the load of a ship in danger.

EXAMPLE:

As the ship filled with seawater, Madame Fontaine pleaded with the sailor not to throw her trunk of clothes overboard with the rest of the **JETSAM** sinking beneath the wild waves.

TRIVIA:

From the 1560s, jetsam is an act of throwing things overboard. In J.R.R. Tolkien's *The Two Towers*, hobbits Merry and Pippin tell the story of how the ents encircled and flooded the tower of Isengard and laid waste to its inhabitants, leaving them to feel like flotsam and jetsam.

MAKE IT STICK:

Using the word *jetsam*, describe a scene in which a sinking ship has cast some bizarre items overboard.

SCHMALTZY
(SHMALT-see), adjective

Overly sentimental (especially with regard to music or art);
tastelessly overdone.

EXAMPLE:

Although Libby loved her
great-grandfather, she found
his **SCHMALTZY** taste
in music hard to bear.

TRIVIA:

First appearing in 1934 from the Yiddish word *shmalts* (rendered chicken
fat or literally "rendered fat"), the
word is informally applied to anything
overly sentimental or corny.

MAKE IT STICK:

Using the word *schmaltzy,* write a short dialogue in which your character
says something overly sentimental to another person.

RAUCOUS
(RAW-kuss), adjective

Rowdy; boisterous; disorderly and wild; harsh or grating to the ear.

EXAMPLE:

My parents' fears that we would use their vacation as an opportunity to stage **RAUCOUS** parties in the den were not entirely without foundation.

TRIVIA:

Bestselling author Elizabeth George summed up *raucous* when she wrote about the "raucous heavy metal of punk guitars screeching like robots put to the rack..."

MAKE IT STICK:

Describe a raucous good time you've had, making sure to use *raucous* in one of your sentences.

EGREGIOUS
(ih-GREE-juss), adjective

Flagrantly incorrect or bad, such as an error that stands out **dramatically**.

EXAMPLE:

Tim, an **EGREGIOUS** liar, is the last person I would go to for reliable information.

TRIVIA:

In the 1530s, *egregious* referred to "distinguished, eminent, excellent" and the now archaic meaning of "remarkably good." Today, *egregious* refers only to shockingly bad errors or errors in judgment.

MAKE IT STICK:

Describe a time when you were given *egregiously* bad information.

GIBBER

(JIB-bur), verb

To speak nervously and incomprehensibly;
to speak in a fast, jumbled, inarticulate manner.

EXAMPLE:

Zack could barely **GIBBER** his way through a conversation with a woman.

TRIVIA:

The first known use of *gibber* was in 1604 and usually refers to rapid, excited, and often nonsensical chatter, such as a baby's babble or other similar jibber-jabber.

MAKE IT STICK:

Write a quick dialogue between two people at a coffee shop, one taciturn and the other *gibbering* away.

FLIBBERTIGIBBET
(FLIB-er-tee-JIBB-it), noun

A chatty, scatterbrained person.

TRIVIA:

Flibbertigibbet became a household word as fans of Rodgers and Hammerstein's 1965 film *The Sound of Music* sang along to "Maria":

How do you find a word that means Maria?
A flibbertigibbet! A will-o'-the wisp! A clown!

MAKE IT STICK:

Incorporate **flibbertigibbet**, *marshmallow*, and *bouquet of roses* into a situation you must endure.

QUANDARY
(KWON-dree), noun

A dilemma; a difficult or uncertain situation.

TRIVIA:

Quandary came to English in the 1570s as a "state of perplexity." Quandaries abound in fiction as protagonists face difficult and uncertain decisions, from Katniss Everdeen in *The Hunger Games* to Sophie Zawistowska in *Sophie's Choice*. Memoirists, such as Tara Westover (*Educated*), often recount the difficult and unfathomable choices they've faced.

MAKE IT STICK:

Finish the scene using the word *quandary*:
It was clear to Francesca that a momentous decision was in front of her. She could push down her uneasy feelings and remain employed at the company or plunge herself into financial uncertainty. She...

EDIFICATION

(ed-ih-fih-KAY-shun), noun

Enlightenment; the process of instructing or sharing important insights.

EXAMPLE:

Although the author includes several supplements on Ancient Egyptian construction methods for the **EDIFICATION** of his readers, they are not directly connected with the book's central idea.

TRIVIA:

Famous showman P.T. Barnum once commented that his circus contained "the wonders of the ages assembled for your edification, education, and enjoyment—for a price."

MAKE IT STICK:

Using *edification,* discuss if you agree with P.T. Barnum about his circus. What things did the circus present to people to enlighten them?

INDUBITABLE

(in-DOO-bih-tuh-bull), adjective

Absolutely unquestionable and completely beyond doubt.

EXAMPLE:

Warren's been right so many times that his judgment is considered **INDUBITABLE**.

TRIVIA:

In the movie *Mary Poppins*, the titular nanny (Julie Andrews) declares that you *can* say supercalifragilisticexpialidocious backward, but adds, "That's going a bit too far, don't you think?" To which Bert (Dick Van Dyke) replies, "Indubitably."

MAKE IT STICK:

Who do you trust so much on a topic that you would deem their expertise *indubitable*? Write about it.

ANDROGYNOUS

(an-DROJ-ih-nuss), adjective

**Neither specifically male nor female;
appearing with both male and female characteristics.**

EXAMPLE:

Amy said her new short haircut was a breeze to maintain compared to the long mane she used to have, but I thought it made her look rather **ANDROGYNOUS**.

TRIVIA:

Some famous people who have embraced both male and female characteristics include musicians Prince, Pink, and David Bowie, actresses Tilda Swinton and Katharine Hepburn, and historical figures such as author Radclyffe Hall and France's fifteenth-century heroine Joan of Arc.

MAKE IT STICK:

Change some characteristics of a protagonist in a book you've read recently to make the character more *androgynous*. Describe the character in four or five sentences.

LAMPOON

(lam-POON), noun, verb

A typically public mean-spirited satire directed at
a person, group, or institution; to mock or ridicule someone.

EXAMPLE:

Many felt Trina's imitation of
Jessica's nervous tic was a cruel
LAMPOON.

TRIVIA:

National Lampoon was a humor mag-
azine that was published from 1970–
1998, which spawned several movies,
radio performances, and live theater
productions. The most famous
of these are the various *National
Lampoon* vacations taken by Chevy
Chase's character Clark Griswold and
National Lampoon's Animal House.

MAKE IT STICK:

Using the word *lampoon,* describe an uncomfortable party scene.

_____

_____

_____

_____

_____

_____

_____

_____

_____

_____

_____

_____

_____

DEBAUCHERY

(dih-BOCH-er-ee), noun

Licentiousness; overindulgent sexual expression; intemperance and immorality with regard to indulgence in physical pleasures.

EXAMPLE:

De Sade's critics claimed they had only to consult his writings for evidence of his **DEBAUCHERY**.

TRIVIA:

Think *National Lampoon's Animal House*, *The Wolf of Wall Street*, HBO's *True Blood*, or fraternity weekends and bachelor parties for a true understanding of overindulging in life's pleasures.

MAKE IT STICK:

Describe a short scene full of *debauchery*.

KIBOSH
(KYE-bosh), noun

The act of halting or squelching (something).

EXAMPLE:

We had wanted to go to the baseball game, but Ryan—who's bored by the sport—put the **KIBOSH** on that.

TRIVIA:

Showing up in the early 1800s, *kibosh*'s origins are still a mystery. What we do know is London's lower class was familiar with it, so Charles Dickens used it (phonetically as *kye-bosh*) in his 1836 collection, *Sketches by Boz*.

MAKE IT STICK:

What are three things your parents put a *kibosh* on when you were growing up?

1. _____

2. _____

3. _____

BOONDOGGLE
(BOON-dahg-uhl), noun

Useless activity designed to make one look busy.

EXAMPLE:

In an effort to appear occupied, Sally filed and re-filed paperwork, but her boss eventually caught on to her **BOONDOGGLE**.

TRIVIA:

Boondoggle was popularized during the New Deal by those who scorned the government programs as providing busywork for the unemployed.

MAKE IT STICK:

Using the word, write about a time you caught someone in the act of a *boondoggle*. What were they doing to trick you into believing they were busy accomplishing something?

_____

_____

_____

_____

_____

_____

_____

_____

BETHINK
(bee-THINK), verb

To cause oneself to consider something; ponder something carefully.

EXAMPLE:

I sat on the porch swing with Grandma on a cool summer night, listening to her **BETHINK** her decision to leave Italy as a teenager and sail to the United States.

TRIVIA:

From the Middle English *bethenken*, this is an antiquated word meaning "to recall." It was used as early as 1819 by poet John Keats and more famously put to use by the Russian writer Leo Tolstoy in his 1904 anti-war text "Bethink Yourselves!"

MAKE IT STICK:

Using *bethink*, describe a short scene in which a soldier or business executive ponders a decision made.

TEETOTALER
(TEE-toe-tuh-ler), noun

Someone who does not drink alcohol under any circumstances.

EXAMPLE:

No wine for me, thanks. I've been a **TEETOTALER** since high school.

MAKE IT STICK:

Write a paragraph using the following: *Sin City, cocktail shaker, Jason, teetotaler,* and *last call.*

TRIVIA:

Though the origin of this word is unclear, it is most likely from the verb *teetotal*, coined during the temperance movement of the nineteenth century. The temperance movement originally addressed hard liquor (beer and wine were fine), but in time came to include all alcohol.

BRIGAND
(BRIG-und), noun

One who lives as a bandit, plundering riches.

EXAMPLE:

The **BRIGANDS** held up the stage-coach and terrified the passengers.

TRIVIA:

The term is believed to have been coined in the late Middle Ages, right about the time Robin Hood emerged as a popular English folk hero sung about in ballads. Robin Hood and his cast of Merry Men stole from the rich and gave to the poor.

MAKE IT STICK:

Write a scene with Robin Hood and his band of Merry Men, incorporating the word *brigand*.

AMALGAM
(uh-MAL-gum), noun

The result of a mixture or combination of two dissimilar things
(as in two breeds of animals or two types of flowers).

EXAMPLE:

Raymond spent all his free time
in the greenhouse perfecting his
beautiful **AMALGAMS** of orchids.

TRIVIA:

In biology, an amalgam is the offspring or result of the combination of
two different breeds, varieties, species, or genera through sexual repro-
duction. Flowers, vegetables, trees,
and numerous animals, such as mules
and ligers (a cross between a male lion
and a female tiger), are all examples.

MAKE IT STICK:

Write a paragraph incorporating the words *amalgam, ranch, Tim,* and *acres.*

MARROW

(MA-row), noun

The tissue filling the cavities
of most bones.

EXAMPLE:

The high-end chef served his guests
MARROW mixed with pâté.

TRIVIA:

It derives from the Old English *mearg*,
which in turn comes from the Old
German *marag*. Marrow in the literal
sense is the tender, fatty insides of
bones. Dogs gnaw to get at the very
best part of a bone, and chefs serve it
as a delicacy. The figurative meaning is
the essence of something, like the marrow of a story, or an inner strength you
might possess in a tough situation.

MAKE IT STICK:

Write two sentences
using the word *marrow* in both its
literal and figurative meanings.

1. _____

_____

_____

2. _____

_____

_____

IMMANENT

(IHM-uh-nant), adjective

Intrinsic, inherent;
existing or operating within.

EXAMPLE:

Dwayne's **IMMANENT** reluctance
to entrust newcomers with tasks
of any significance was a major
problem for the company.

TRIVIA:

Immanent is from the 1500s, deriving
from the Latin *immanēre*, meaning "to
remain in place." It is not to be confused
with *imminent*, which means "close at
hand, as in death or danger."

MAKE IT STICK:

What are three things of which you have
an *immanent* distrust?

1. _____

2. _____

3. _____

RAVENOUS

(RAV-uh-nuss), adjective

Powerfully hungry; intensely eager to be satisfied.

EXAMPLE:

I am **RAVENOUS**; fortunately dinner will be served soon.

TRIVIA:

Ravenous has its roots in the late fourteenth century, at the time meaning "obsessed with plundering, extremely greedy" from the Old French *ravine*, meaning "violent rush, robbery." By the early fifteenth century, the term shifted to meaning "voracious." Interestingly enough, the word has nothing to do with ravens.

MAKE IT STICK:

Finish the scene using the word *ravenous*:
Sheryl stared at her grandson as he ate the slice of pizza in three bites, silently thanking the restaurant for cutting the pizza into twelve slices...

_____

_____

_____

_____

_____

_____

_____

_____

_____

_____

_____

_____

QUELL
(kwell), verb

To subdue; to crush or extinguish; to overcome.

EXAMPLE:

The firemen sought to **QUELL** the rapidly spreading blaze but, due to equipment malfunctions, were unable to do so.

TRIVIA:

Another gory beginning—it comes from the Old English *cwellan*, meaning "to kill, murder, execute." The use of the word as "to suppress or subdue" came along around the 1300s. The famous line from John Dryden's 1687 poem "A Song for St. Cecilia's Day" states, "What passion cannot music raise and quell?"

MAKE IT STICK:

Write three sentences incorporating *quell*—one meaning to subdue a crowd, one to subdue a fire, and one to subdue an emotion.

1. _____
_____

2. _____
_____

3. _____
_____

LACKADAISICAL
(lack-uh-DAZE-ih-kul), adjective

Lacking spirit or energy; languid.

EXAMPLE:

I was feeling rather **LACKADAISICAL** last Sunday, so I stayed in bed all day and watched football instead of mowing the lawn.

TRIVIA:

Lackadaisical dates back to the 1600s when people who were having a bad day would exclaim, "Alack the day!" It was shortened to *lackaday*, and in the mid-1700s the term *lackadaisical* was coined to describe how one feels when things just aren't going your way.

MAKE IT STICK:

Describe a time you were *lackadaisical*.

_____
_____
_____
_____
_____
_____
_____
_____
_____
_____

STODGY
(STAHJ-ee), adjective

Dull, uninteresting, and tediously commonplace.

EXAMPLE:

I could only spend five minutes in the **STODGY** club before I left for a rowdier place.

TRIVIA:

Originally meaning "thick, semi-solid" when it first appeared in 1823, *stodgy* took on the meaning of "dull, heavy" in 1874. The British use of *stodgy* also includes food characteristics, as in a stodgy cake (perhaps a dense fruitcake), which probably isn't preferable to a light, fluffy layer cake with whipped icing!

MAKE IT STICK:

Use *stodgy* in two different scenarios:
first, to describe a place you're stuck spending the afternoon,
and second, to describe a stodgy food you were forced to consume.

FOUR-FLUSHER
(FOR-flush-ur), noun

In poker, a player who bluffs.

EXAMPLE:

Our Friday night poker games aren't for novices; everyone involved is an experienced **FOUR-FLUSHER**.

TRIVIA:

Used in poker, *four-flusher* is derived from the 1896 verb *four-flush*, meaning "to bluff a poker hand" by claiming to hold five cards of one suit while only holding four (this assumes a game in which the jokers are wild). The word is used generally to mean "someone who is bluffing."

MAKE IT STICK:

Using the word *four-flusher,* describe a scene in which you could bluff someone and they'd believe what you're saying.

SYCOPHANTIC
(sih-koh-FAN-tik), adjective

Obsequious; seeking to curry favor.

EXAMPLE:

There was no need to be so **SYCOPHANTIC** to the judge; the hearing was just over a parking ticket.

TRIVIA:

In ancient Greece, *sykophantēs* meant "slanderer." *Sykon* is the Greek word for "fig" and *phainein* means "to show, make known." The term was originally a vulgar gesture and applied to those who informed on criminal activities.

MAKE IT STICK:

Finish the scene incorporating the word *sycophantic*: Jean sat in the conference room, listening to her colleague gush over the new CEO...

MALINGER
(muh-LING-ger), verb

To avoid work by making up excuses.

EXAMPLE:

"There will be no **MALINGERING** in this office," the new supervisor said sternly.

TRIVIA:

First coined in English in 1820 as "to pretend illness to escape duty," *malingering* these days also includes exaggerating or making up physical or psychological ailments to avoid work, obtain financial compensation like disability pay, or circumvent criminal prosecution.

MAKE IT STICK:

Finish the acrostic with ways someone could avoid work:

M _____

A _____

L _____

I _____

N _____

G _____

E _____

R _____

RUBBERNECK

(RUH-bur-nek), verb

To watch intently;
to gaze at in fascination.

EXAMPLE:

Traffic slowed near the crash on the other side of the highway due to people **RUBBERNECKING.**

TRIVIA:

Rubberneck first appeared in the 1890s and has come to mean "staring at something in an exaggerated manner," perhaps craning one's head to see as many details as possible.

MAKE IT STICK:

Using the word *rubberneck*, describe the traffic and your experience as you pass a crash by the side of the road.

_____

_____

_____

_____

_____

_____

_____

_____

FERVENT

(FER-vunt), adjective

Ardent and enthusiastic.
Literally, extremely hot.

EXAMPLE:

Russell's speech was characterized by **FERVENT** emotion.

TRIVIA:

From the Old French *fervent*, meaning "fervent, ardent," and the Latin *ferventem*, meaning "boiling, hot, glowing," the word has meant "a strong, passionate devotion," as in a fervent desire.

MAKE IT STICK:

What are you *fervent* about? Describe it.

_____

_____

_____

_____

_____

_____

_____

_____

_____

_____

MAWKISH
(MAW-kish), adjective

Overly sentimental; maudlin.

EXAMPLE:

Daytime soap operas irritated Melanie; she found them **MAWKISH** and unbelievable.

TRIVIA:

Mawk derives from the Middle English word for "maggot" and turned up in the 1660s with the meaning of "something nauseating or sickly." The figurative meaning of "sickeningly sentimental" started to take hold in 1702.

MAKE IT STICK:

Write a few sentences describing something overly sentimental using *mawkish, bumper sticker, Darnell,* and *acid rock.*

INTERJECTION
(ihn-ter-JEK-shun), noun

An exclamation, interruption, or oath;
an action or remark that interrupts.

EXAMPLE:

When I tried to take the last brownie
from the platter, I was met with
a myriad of **INTERJECTIONS**
from my friends.

TRIVIA:

As the *Schoolhouse Rock!* ditty suggests, interjections are exclamations that show excitement and emotion! Their use has multiplied in the age of electronic communication. Abbreviations such as LOL and OMG form interjections in text messages.

MAKE IT STICK:

Create a some-assembly-required scene where you use the word *interjection*.

RANKLE
(RANG-kul), verb

To cause irritation or festering resentment.

EXAMPLE:

The criticism he received for his plan **RANKLED** Paul for some time.

TRIVIA:

Benjamin Franklin once said, "If you argue and rankle and contradict, you may achieve a temporary victory—sometimes; but it will be an empty victory because you will never get your opponent's good will."

MAKE IT STICK:

Finish the scene using *rankle*:
Annie stared at the third rejection letter she'd received that day. "Despite having lots of really good material here, I just don't think…"

VITRIOLIC
(vit-ree-OL-ik), adjective

Acidic (literally, but also in tone); harsh and caustic.

EXAMPLE:

McCarthy's **VITRIOLIC** attacks on organizations with no actual Communist ties went largely unchallenged in the Senate.

TRIVIA:

In *The Rutherford Report*'s "Civility in Political Discourse," there is the comment, "When political disagreements spark vitriolic rhetoric, the result is deeper divisions that lessen the probability of compromise and cooperation, which are also essential to our democratic process." Most vitriolic speeches have the intent to divide or degrade rather than seek resolution.

MAKE IT STICK:

Write a scene where you or a character receives a *vitriolic* letter.

EMINENT

(EM-ih-nunt), adjective

Prominent or noted; of high esteem; outstanding and distinguished.

EXAMPLE:

I found the prospect of studying physics under an **EMINENT** professor like Dr. Maxwell, who'd just won a Nobel Prize, daunting to say the least.

TRIVIA:

In use since the early fifteenth century, *eminent* is something "standing or rising above" and can refer to a place or a person.

MAKE IT STICK:

Who are five *eminent* women of the last century and why?

1. _____

2. _____

3. _____

4. _____

5. _____

CUMBROUS

(KUM-bruss), adjective

Hard to handle or manage.

EXAMPLE:

The deliveryman had a tough time getting that **CUMBROUS** package to our front door.

TRIVIA:

By the fifteenth century, *cumbrous* meant "difficult to handle or awkward because of shape or size."

MAKE IT STICK:

Write a sentence or two using the following: *Christmas tree*, **cumbrous**, *Frank*, and *hernia*.

_____
_____
_____
_____
_____
_____
_____
_____
_____
_____
_____
_____
_____

LOGY
(LOW-ghee), adjective

Lethargic or sluggish.

EXAMPLE:

On really cold days, my already **LOGY** car absolutely refuses to start.

TRIVIA:

With its uncertain origin, *logy* might have come from the Dutch word *log*, meaning "heavy." It was first used in print in an 1847 London newspaper article that referred to a "loggy stroke" in rowing.

MAKE IT STICK:

Write a short scene or paragraph incorporating
logy, *weather*, *Julie*, and *fireplace*.

OXYMORON
(ahk-see-MORE-on), noun

A phrase in which contradictory or incongruous terms are used together, as in the phrase "poor little rich kid."

EXAMPLE:

When Ted said the term *military intelligence* always struck him as an **OXYMORON**, he meant it as a joke, but his cousin, a lifelong army officer, took grave offense.

TRIVIA:

From the Greek *oxymoron*, meaning "pointedly foolish," *oxymoron* has morphed to mean word combinations that are often humorous contradictions, like *deafening silence*, *jumbo shrimp*, *clearly confused*, and *original copy*.

MAKE IT STICK:

Write a short dialogue between friends in which one or both of them state something contradictory or incongruous. Be sure to incorporate the word *oxymoron*.

WINSOME
(WIN-sum), adjective

Pleasant; charming.

EXAMPLE:

Although he had overslept and been in a rush to get out of the house, a **WINSOME** glance from the vaguely familiar woman at the toll collection booth helped put Milton's morning back on track.

TRIVIA:

Scotland's national poet Robert "Rabbie" Burns is loved the world over for his poems encompassing themes of love and nature. He wrote this charming ditty:

> She is a winsome wee thing,
> She is a handsome wee thing,
> She is a lo'esome wee thing,
> This sweet wee wife o' mine.

MAKE IT STICK:

Write a short scene or paragraph incorporating the following:
winsome, curls, Maxine, and *soda fountain.*

CARBUNCLE

(KAR-bunk-uhl), noun

A painful inflammation of the skin similar to, but more serious than, a boil.

EXAMPLE:

Jimmy's inventive excuses for his absences reached a new level when he told his teacher he'd been unable to attend Spanish class because of a **CARBUNCLE**.

TRIVIA:

Carbuncle started off in the early thirteenth century meaning "a gem," literally a gem of deep garnet hue. The term morphed to mean something quite undesirable—a red, inflamed spot—within just a couple hundred years.

MAKE IT STICK:

Using *carbuncle* in a sentence, describe a scene in which a vain person wakes up with a carbuncle on his/her face.

_____

_____

_____

_____

_____

_____

_____

XANADU

(ZAN-uh-doo), noun

A place of great beauty and luxury.

EXAMPLE:

The Caribbean resort, with its palm trees and ocean breezes, was a **XANADU** of earthly delights.

TRIVIA:

Xanadu is a Mongol city founded by Kublai Khan in the 1620s. The use of it as a "dream place of magnificence and luxury" comes from Samuel Taylor Coleridge's 1816 poem "Kubla Khan." It is also the title of a 1977 song by Rush and the 1980 musical fantasy film starring Olivia Newton-John.

MAKE IT STICK:

Describe your own *Xanadu*!

_____

_____

_____

_____

_____

_____

_____

PHILTER
(FIL-tur), noun

A magical love potion.

TRIVIA:

This "love potion" term comes from the late 1500s, amidst the frenzy of witch hunting. No doubt someone was feeling amorous toward another and, instead of blaming it on the wine, decided to add a little mystery to it.

MAKE IT STICK:

Write a scene incorporating the following:
philter, kiosk, Danny, and *guitar strings.*

GUFFAW
(guh-FAW), noun, verb

An instance of full,
unrestrained laughter.

EXAMPLE:

From the howls and **GUFFAWS**
I heard issuing from the auditorium,
I gathered the principal's speech
introducing a new dress code for the
school was not going well.

TRIVIA:

Attributed to the Scots and first
noted in 1720, the term borders on
onomatopoeia—you can almost hear the
sound of deep belly laughter in the word.

MAKE IT STICK:

Write a situation in which you
or a character *guffaws*.

CANTANKEROUS
(kan-TANG-ker-us), adjective

Ill-tempered; grumpy.

EXAMPLE:

"You kids stay off my lawn!" our
CANTANKEROUS old neighbor barked.

TRIVIA:

If they had such a thing back then,
Ebenezer Scrooge would have been
voted "most likely to become cantankerous" in his high school yearbook. Of
course, that was before the visit from
the Ghost of Christmas Yet to Come,
but his spiteful and noxious attitude
definitely made him someone with
whom no one wanted to spend much
time.

MAKE IT STICK:

Who's your favorite *cantankerous* character of all time? Using the word, describe
something specific the character does
that makes him or her cantankerous.

POTAGE

(PO-taj), noun

A thick soup usually involving chicken stock, cheese,
and white wine—possibly also chicken.

TRIVIA:

Originating in France, potage gets
its name from the thick crockery in
which it's cooked (the name literally
means "potted meal"). Though foreigners may prefer something more
delicate, potage is a staple of virtu-
ally every French kitchen.

MAKE IT STICK:

Write a recipe with humorous directive steps
for making *potage* out of oats, wheat, rye, or rice.

ONOMATOPOEIA
(on-uh-mot-uh-PEE-uh), noun

The development of a word whose pronunciation imitates
its main reference, such as *splat* and *buzz*.

EXAMPLE:

Over the centuries, the use of
ONOMATOPOEIA has become an
accepted part of the English language.

TRIVIA:

While this is a word you don't want
to get in a spelling bee, the concept
of onomatopoeia is very simple—a
word that conjures up a sound. A
great example of its use is Edgar
Allan Poe's poem "The Bells":

> *Yet the ear, it fully knows,*
> *By the twanging*
> *And the clanging,*
> *How the danger ebbs and flows.*

MAKE IT STICK:

Write out a restaurant scene using words that conjure up the sounds
of what's happening in the kitchen as food is being prepared.
Be sure to use the word *onomatopoeia*.

INTERREGNUM
(in-ter-REG-num), noun

The period between one ruler and another.

EXAMPLE:

The **INTERREGNUM**—which lasted several months—was filled with work and planning by the palace staff.

TRIVIA:

Coming from Latin *inter-* meaning "between" and *regnum* meaning "dominion, rule," the word gained a more precise meaning during the time between when Charles I of England was beheaded in 1649 and 1660 when, after the death of Oliver Cromwell, Parliament invited Charles II to return from exile in France.

MAKE IT STICK:

Write a sentence or short paragraph using the words *interregnum*, *politics*, and *lost heir*.

TRUMPERY
(TRUMP-uh-ree), noun

Worthless stuff; a thing or things without value; nonsense.

MAKE IT STICK:

You are clearing your garage with your spouse or partner. Using the word *trumpery*, describe a disagreement over what is pitched and what is kept.

LIONIZE

(LIE-uh-nize), verb

To praise excessively; to idolize.

EXAMPLE:

For years, young baseball fans **LIONIZED** Babe Ruth, whose many indiscretions were usually overlooked by the press.

TRIVIA:

Lionize was used in the early 1700s to refer to a sought-after famous individual, and it's believed this use is derived from the lions once kept at the famed Tower of London. These lions and the menagerie of which they were a part generated great curiosity and were a must-see for visitors to London—hence the original use of *lionize* seems to be "seeking out objects of fascination" or, quite literally, lions.

MAKE IT STICK:

Admit it:
What celebrity do you *lionize* and why?

_____
_____
_____
_____
_____
_____
_____

CAVALIER

(ka-vuh-LEER), adjective

Snobbishly offhand.

EXAMPLE:

I tried to apologize for bumping into the woman, but she only gave me a **CAVALIER** glance and inspected her fur coat for damage.

TRIVIA:

In sixteenth-century England, during the English Civil War, the Puritan opponents of Charles I applied the term disdainfully to Charles's supporters.

MAKE IT STICK:

Who are your five favorite *cavalier* characters from books, shows, or movies?

1. _____

2. _____

3. _____

4. _____

5. _____

IMBROGLIO
(im-BROA-lee-o), noun

An entanglement or complicated misunderstanding;
a delicate situation from which it is difficult to extricate oneself.

EXAMPLE:

The recent **IMBROGLIO** over conflict-of-interest violations hasn't improved the mayor's standing with voters.

TRIVIA:

Imbroglio and *embroilment* are entangled in their meaning. English speakers adopted the French *embroil* early in the seventeenth century. By the mid-1700s it had merged with the Italian *imbrogliare* to form *imbroglio*, meaning "a complicated misunderstanding or entanglement," such as when your wife and mistress show up to dinner at the same time.

MAKE IT STICK:

Incorporating *imbroglio,* describe a humorous mix-up at a family holiday dinner.

PRATTLE
(PRAT-ul), noun

Meaningless babble; idle chatter.

EXAMPLE:

I stopped at the diner to have breakfast and read the morning paper, but the endless **PRATTLE** of the waitress made it impossible for me to get beyond the front page.

TRIVIA:

In the 1980s sitcom *Cheers*, Frasier counsels Woody on how to deal with a customer who blabbers: "People in this situation have a tendency to prattle on endlessly, totally unaware of how others are receiving this unwanted, innocuous information."

MAKE IT STICK:

Finish the scene incorporating *prattle*:
The four-year-old twins sat across from each other at the miniature picnic table, the box of crayons dumped out between them...

QUAGMIRE
(KWAG-mire), noun

An entanglement that offers no ready solution or means of escape. Literally, a boggy patch of ground that wagons and caravans often cannot pass over.

EXAMPLE:

The hostage situation now threatens to become the worst **QUAGMIRE** of this administration.

TRIVIA:

Quagmire's original meaning of "bog or marsh" in the 1570s extended to an inescapable bad position by 1766. It was not in common use but received a bit of a revival in David Halberstam's 1965 book *The Making of a Quagmire*, a reference to military invasions.

MAKE IT STICK:

Write two sentences incorporating *quagmire,* one using its literal meaning of a boggy patch and one describing a figurative entanglement.

1. _____
_____
_____

2. _____
_____
_____

PANACHE
(puh-NASH), noun

A distinctive flair or style; a flamboyant manner.

EXAMPLE:

Rosamund was swept away by the charming stranger's **PANACHE**—he seemed so dashing and romantic.

TRIVIA:

In the Canadian sitcom *Schitt's Creek* (the first show to ever sweep all four acting categories at the Emmy Awards, as another piece of trivia), once wealthy but always eccentric parents, Johnny and Moira, lead the Rose family in their panache, from wigs and Italian wingtips to designer outfits and unique public personas.

MAKE IT STICK:

Describe someone with *panache.*

_____
_____
_____
_____
_____
_____

TANDEM
(TAN-dum), adjective

One after another, as in a single file line.

EXAMPLE:

We gave Mom and Dad a **TANDEM** bicycle for Christmas this year.

TRIVIA:

While things done in tandem are usually positive, on the TV show *Scrubs*, Dr. Cox tells Dr. Kelso that his ex-wife would "be there waiting for me in the afterlife. You see, typical of her, she went ahead and signed us up for an eternal tandem bike ride all along the banks of the River Styx."

MAKE IT STICK:

Finish the scene using *tandem*: Beth and Gene thought renting bikes would be a fun way to see Nantucket, but when they arrived at the rental shop...

MOTLEY
(MOT-lee), adjective

Of diverse composition, such as showing many colors or facets.

EXAMPLE:

It was Frederick's job to mold the **MOTLEY** assemblage he'd been given into a powerful fighting force.

TRIVIA:

The word has come to carry negative overtones of raggedness or lack of union. In the late 1300s, *motley* was used to describe cloth with contrasting colors and then shifted to meaning "fool" in 1600, perhaps after a jester's garb.

MAKE IT STICK:

Write a short sentence or paragraph using *motley*, *fishing pole*, and *vampire*.

CLOUT

(klowt), noun, verb

Someone with a lot of extra-legal influence; to strike someone.

EXAMPLE:

I was afraid we wouldn't get into the exclusive club, but Reggie's business connections give him a lot of **CLOUT**. We got in without a problem.

TRIVIA:

The slang meaning of "extra-legal influence" was adopted in 1946. American actress, Kathy Bates, said of clout, "People are always saying, 'Well, you go to Hollywood and you get yourself a film career or a TV series, and then you can do anything you want. Because then you've got the clout.' That had always sounded like a lot of hooey to me, but now I think it's true, unfortunately."

MAKE IT STICK:

Write two sentences using both meanings of *clout*—one referring to extra-legal influence and one where someone is struck.

1. _____

_____

2. _____

_____

LARGESSE

(lahr-JESS), noun

Generosity, especially with money.

EXAMPLE:

My parents' **LARGESSE** dried up after I asked them for money three months in a row.

TRIVIA:

This term has been in use since at least the thirteenth century and derives from the French word for "abundant."

MAKE IT STICK:

Write a sentence or short paragraph incorporating *largesse, will,* and your *late Uncle Alfred.*

_____
_____
_____
_____
_____
_____
_____
_____
_____
_____
_____
_____
_____

CONCOURSE
(KON-korss), noun

A large crowd; an open space or hall, such as
an airport terminal, where crowds gather.

TRIVIA:
This word derives from the Latin
concourre by way of Middle French
and Middle English. It arrived at its
current sense in the mid-nineteenth
century. It is also the name of a computer automation system.

MAKE IT STICK:

Finish the scene using *concourse*:
Andy circled around the block, trying to get closer to the commotion in the street...

SONOROUS
(SON-uh-russ), adjective

Deep or rich in sound; overblown or conceited in language.

EXAMPLE:

The chairman's **SONOROUS** but mercifully brief remarks brought the long meeting to a close.

TRIVIA:

While *sonorous* most often describes sound and speech, Impressionist painter Pierre-Auguste Renoir said of art and color, "I want a red to be sonorous, to sound like a bell. If it doesn't turn out that way, I add more reds and other colors until I get it."

MAKE IT STICK:

Write a paragraph incorporating *sonorous* along with *Katie, fog, church bells,* and *graveyard.*

WANGLE
(WANG-gul), verb

To get one's own way by using manipulation or clever means.

EXAMPLE:

Franz **WANGLED** two tickets to the concert by pretending to be the son of the city's premier entertainment critic.

TRIVIA:

The term came to English as slang and was used by English printers in the 1880s when they used photographic trickery to make images look like something they weren't—an early version of Photoshop!

MAKE IT STICK:

Finish this scene using the word *wangle*: Megan couldn't understand how she'd managed to be nominated for the neighborhood beatification committee...

HIDEBOUND
(HIDE-bound), adjective

Narrow and rigid in one's beliefs or opinions.

EXAMPLE:

I wouldn't mind Mary's **HIDEBOUND** beliefs if she didn't share them so freely!

TRIVIA:

Originally used in an agricultural sense to refer to cattle with dry, cracking skin, it morphed into use as stingy or miserly but is now used to describe people who are unyielding in their beliefs and actions. Think of it as a polite way to call someone stubborn.

MAKE IT STICK:

Finish the scene incorporating the word *hidebound*: John should have known better than to wear his NRA shirt to his grandmother's house.

RAPPORT
(rah-POR), noun

A natural liking or affection
for something or someone;
a harmonious relationship.

EXAMPLE:
The king had a **RAPPORT** for those on
his council who always said he was right.

TRIVIA:
As you might expect, this comes from
the French *rapporter*, which came from
the Latin *apportare*, meaning "to bring
or to carry."

MAKE IT STICK:
List five different things with
which you have a *rapport*:

1. _____

2. _____

3. _____

4. _____

5. _____

PRUDENT
(PROOD-nt), adjective

Exercising due care with
regard to one's interests;
judiciously considered.

EXAMPLE:
I believe the merger was a **PRUDENT**
course of action, one that will solidify
our cash position immediately.

TRIVIA:
In the sitcom *The Big Bang Theory*, Barry
Kripke asks Sheldon if he's afraid of
heights. Sheldon responds, "Hardly. A fear
of heights is illogical. Fear of falling, on the
other hand, is prudent and evolutionary."

MAKE IT STICK:
Incorporating the word *prudent,*
describe a time when you took judicious
care in your actions.

_____

_____

_____

_____

_____

_____

_____

_____

_____

_____

DEBONAIR
(deb-uh-NAIR), adjective

Suave; sophisticated and charming.

EXAMPLE:

Paul's **DEBONAIR** manner never abandoned him, even at the most difficult moments.

TRIVIA:

From the French for "of good lineage." Used in Middle English to mean "docile, courteous," *debonair* was revived to mean "pleasantly light-hearted and affable" by the 1680s.

MAKE IT STICK:

Write a short paragraph using *debonair* with this prompt: Trish tapped her watch impatiently while Chip examined himself in the mirror...

TORTE
(tort), noun

A cake made with eggs
and very little flour.
(Distinct from *tort*, a legal term.)

EXAMPLE:

Mrs. Carrigan's Linzer **TORTES** are the
best I've ever tasted.

TRIVIA:

While cakes and tortes are similar, they
are not the same. Cakes are usually
made with sugar, eggs, butter, and flour.
Tortes, on the other hand, use much less
flour, substituting ground nuts or bread
crumbs instead.

MAKE IT STICK:

Write a **sentence** or two incorporating the
following: *teacup, torte, Sonja,* and *cafe.*

_____

_____

_____

_____

_____

_____

_____

_____

DISGRUNTLEMENT
(dis-GRUN-tul-ment), noun

A feeling of brooding discontent;
evidence of disappointment and
disquiet with oneself.

EXAMPLE:

The instant rejection of my application led
to an unshakable **DISGRUNTLEMENT**
that I would never get a job.

TRIVIA:

This word first appears in 1682, its root
the Middle English *gruntlen*, meaning "to
grunt." There is no positive form "grun-
tle," though various comedic writers have
used it. Sadly, you can't be gruntled with
yourself for learning this word!

MAKE IT STICK:

Describe a scenario that would cause
disgruntlement using the words *red
wine, mother,* and *family business.*

_____

_____

_____

_____

_____

_____

_____

HUBRIS
(HYOO-briss), noun

Excessive pride. Can refer to the "fatal flaw" of ancient Greek drama or to any disproportionate pride or self-love.

EXAMPLE:

Colin may have begun as a pleasant and unassuming clerk, but by the time he took over the company in 2018 he showed signs of the **HUBRIS** that would accompany his downfall.

TRIVIA:

Famous literary characters exuding hubris are Shakespeare's Macbeth, F. Scott Fitzgerald's Jay Gatsby, and Sophocles's Oedipus.

MAKE IT STICK:

Who are three sports figures for whom you feel *hubris* brought about a shortened career?

1. _____

2. _____

3. _____

SQUALOR
(SKWAL-ur), noun

The state or quality of being filthy.

EXAMPLE:

My mother knew full well that my roommates were not the tidiest men in the world, but she still seemed shocked when confronted with the unrepentant **SQUALOR** of our apartment.

TRIVIA:

Squalor appeared in English in the 1620s and derives from the Latin *squalēre*, meaning "to be filthy." *Squalor* can be used in the exaggerated sense, like a dirty apartment.

MAKE IT STICK:

Let's use *squalor* in its literal sense. Describe Wilbur's pigpen from *Charlotte's Web* or an apartment that has been abused by partygoers.

_____

_____

_____

_____

_____

_____

_____

_____

DELL
(dell), noun

A small wooded valley; a glen.

EXAMPLE:

I emerged from the tent in the wee hours of the morning to find a sand-colored doe peering at me from the edge of the **DELL**.

TRIVIA:

While *dell* doesn't come up in everyday conversation, it has remained in use for the past two hundred years thanks to the nursery rhyme "The Farmer in the Dell."

MAKE IT STICK:

Describe a picnic scene on the edge of a *dell*.

BUFFOONERY
(buh-FOON-er-ee), noun

A comedy in which a situation, satire, and preposterous coincidence are predominant over character; a ridiculous, empty display not worth serious consideration; a mockery.

EXAMPLE:

Although the proceedings were presented to the outside world as a fair trial, Roland knew he was watching a **BUFFOONERY** in which all the principal witnesses had been bribed to help convict the defendant.

TRIVIA:

Buffare in Italian means "to puff out one's cheeks." This was the style of Italian clowns in the seventeenth century, so by extension the word came to mean "behave like a clown."

MAKE IT STICK:

Describe a few examples in which actors got themselves into farcical situations. Be sure to use the word *buffoonery*.

HINTERLAND
(HIN-tur-land), noun

An area far away from the coastline; an area far removed from a city.

EXAMPLE:

The blizzard dumped nearly three feet of snow on my relatives in the **HINTERLAND**, while those of us in town had to deal with icy rain and flooding.

TRIVIA:

Geographer George Chisholm borrowed the German term *hinterland* in 1888 to describe the region inland from a port or coastal settlement. Today, *hinterland* can mean an area outside a city area (to which it is economically tied) and also land that's out in the middle of nowhere.

MAKE IT STICK:

Finish the scene incorporating *hinterland*: Stars blazed in the night sky and fireflies lit up the field. Nandini was amazed she hadn't thought to vacation here before.

HIBACHI
(hih-BOCH-ee), noun

A small, tabletop charcoal grill.

EXAMPLE:

The manager of the apartment complex wouldn't allow tenants to keep full-sized gas or charcoal grills on the balconies, but she did make occasional allowances for **HIBACHIS**.

TRIVIA:

Hibachi combines the Japanese words *hi* for "fire" and *hachi* for "bowl or pot," and they are just that—small portable bowls used to hold charcoal and cook outdoors. The small portable grill was popular among post-Word War II suburban families that wanted to enjoy outdoor cooking.

MAKE IT STICK:

Grill it up! Describe a scene in which you're cooking dinner on a *hibachi*.

PLACARD
(PLACK-urd), noun

A notice or sign set out on stiff paper or board.

MAKE IT STICK:

Write a scene set at the airport using the word *placard*.

_____

_____

_____

_____

_____

_____

_____

_____

_____

_____

_____

_____

_____

_____

FESTOON
(feh-STOON), noun, verb

**A garland strung between two points;
to decorate as with garlands.**

EXAMPLE:

Balloons and banners **FESTOONED** the room in anticipation of my son's birthday party.

TRIVIA:

The term *festoon* probably comes from the Italian word *festone*, meaning "feast." A feast is the perfect event in which to string up garlands of flowers. *Festoon* is both a noun (the garland) and verb (the act of hanging the garland).

MAKE IT STICK:

Using the word *festoon*, describe a scene in which you are decorating for a fiftieth wedding anniversary.

REMUNERATIVE

(rih-MYOON-er-uh-tive),
adjective

Profitable; providing compensation.

EXAMPLE:

Jane quit her day job after she found her online business was more **REMUNERATIVE** than she'd expected.

TRIVIA:

First used in English in the late 1600s to mean "rewarding," by the mid-1800s the definition had shifted to "profitable." *Remunerative* can also refer to something that generates a lot of money.

MAKE IT STICK:

Write a few sentences about a job or situation that is more *remunerative* than you thought it would be.

_____

_____

_____

_____

_____

_____

_____

_____

_____

_____

FABULIST

(FAB-yuh-list), noun

A liar; someone who tells outrageously untrue stories.

EXAMPLE:

Sir Gerald, a notorious **FABULIST**, was not consulted for an authoritative account of the crime.

TRIVIA:

The word *fabulist* goes back to the 1590s and derives from the Latin *fābula*, meaning "story" or "tale," and the Old French *fable*, meaning "lie or pretense."

MAKE IT STICK:

List three characters from TV who are *fabulists*.

1. _____

2. _____

3. _____

DEBUTANTE

(DEB-yoo-tont), noun

A young woman making her debut into society; any unmarried young woman perceived to move in high social circles.

EXAMPLE:

Molly and her friends scanned the newspaper's society column for a review of their **DEBUTANTE** ball.

TRIVIA:

The term *debutante* was introduced in 1801 to mean a "female stage actress making her first public performance." The practice of young women being introduced to society, often in the form of a ball, began in the 1600s with women of high society or noble birth. Though the word is French, the tradition of debutante balls exists almost entirely in the English-speaking world. In the United States, the tradition is still carried on, even if it is declining in popularity. The UK outlawed them in 1958.

MAKE IT STICK:

Describe a *debutante* in all her glory, à la *Gone with the Wind*.

APOSTATE
(uh-POS-tate), noun

A person who professes belief in a dogma or system of belief (especially a religion) but differs with a tenet of that system; often used more loosely to describe a member of a group or organization who airs opinions that conflict with established principles or routines.

EXAMPLE:

His stand against the agency's involvement in Guatemala led some to brand Clint an **APOSTATE**.

TRIVIA:

Coming from the Greek *apostátēs*, meaning "runaway" (specifically "runaway slave"), the word has a long tradition. In the fourth century, when Roman emperor Julian sought to break with Christianity and return to worship of the old Roman gods, he became known as Julian the Apostate.

MAKE IT STICK:

Using the word *apostate*, finish this paragraph:
The meeting came to an abrupt halt when Amanda, the acting president, snorted as she read the group's code of ethics.

RESTITUTION

(res-ti-TOO-shun), noun

**The act of compensating for a past misdeed;
the acknowledgment of the wrongness of a past act
and attempt to repair the damage caused by it.**

EXAMPLE:

A bill authorizing **RESTITUTION** to the citizens interned in the camps recently cleared Congress.

MAKE IT STICK:

Using the word *restitution,* write about a current situation you feel warrants some kind of restitution.

TRIVIA:

Probably the youngest child, albeit fictional, to ever demand restitution is Charles Schulz's Sally Brown. In the 1966 made-for-television Halloween special *It's the Great Pumpkin, Charlie Brown,* Sally spends Halloween night with Linus waiting for the Great Pumpkin. She laments, "Trick or treats come only once a year, and I missed it by sitting in a pumpkin patch with a blockhead. *You owe me restitution!*"

SPIEL
(shpeel), noun

A long, extravagant argument or speech designed to persuade.

EXAMPLE:

I let the salesman recite his **SPIEL** just to be polite, but the guy impressed me so much I ended up buying a vacuum cleaner after all.

TRIVIA:

The word first appeared in 1870 from the German *spielen*, meaning "to play," but has been used to mean "glib speech, pitch" since 1896. While spiel was originally just a game, it's now an integral part of many sales pitches!

MAKE IT STICK:

Using the word *spiel*, finish this scene: Sandra opened the door to find three Girl Scouts standing on her porch holding boxes of cookies. "Well, go ahead," she said. "Let me have it."

AUDACIOUS
(ow-DAY-shuss), adjective

Bold or shameless in display; unconcerned with the reactions of others.

EXAMPLE:

None of us understood how Julia and Ted, each of whom is married, could have been so **AUDACIOUS** about their romance.

TRIVIA:

The word first appeared in the 1500s and comes from the Latin *audāx*, meaning "boldness." It acquired a negative connotation by the 1590s, but today it is mostly positive.

MAKE IT STICK:

Finish the scene using *audacious*: Sue didn't have a problem telling the cop to pull over when he entered the stadium parking lot through the wrong gate...

PORTENTOUS
(por-TEN-shuss), adjective

Foreboding or menacing; foretelling the possibility of future harm or evil.

EXAMPLE:

The day began with sunny weather, but by 2 p.m. a **PORTENTOUS** sky threatened to ruin our outing.

TRIVIA:

The word originated in the 1540s and has its roots in the word *portents*. To the ancient Romans, portents, or omens, were very important, and much of the work of Roman priests was slaughtering animals in order to read omens from their entrails.

MAKE IT STICK:

Using the words *portentous, lightning,* and *lake,* write one or two sentences describing an ominous scene.

GOSSAMER

(GOSS-uh-mer), adjective

Light, delicate, and tenuous;
reminiscent of a floating film of cobwebs.

EXAMPLE:

Some mornings, the grass outside our house sports a **GOSSAMER** veil.

MAKE IT STICK:

Using the word *gossamer*, describe a scene involving a fairy, troll, and meadow.

TRIVIA:

Gossamer dates to the 1300s but has a somewhat ambiguous history. There's some evidence the word is derived from *gos* (goose) and *sumer* (summer), which might reference the silky down of a goose. More likely it refers to late goose summer, a warm spell in October and November, which was when people felt geese were best for eating. Cobwebs also tended to float in the calm, clear autumn air, so that gets to the idea of light, delicate, and gossamer-like qualities, as in a light, airy fabric.

NEFARIOUS

(nih-FARE-ee-uss), adjective

Openly evil; wicked.

EXAMPLE:

The **NEFARIOUS** Darth Vader serves as the unforgettable villain of George Lucas's Star Wars series.

TRIVIA:

From the early 1600s and meaning "wicked in the extreme," the word hasn't changed much over the years. Comic book superheroes, John McClane in the *Die Hard* movies, and Eliot Ness of the real-life Untouchables all took on nefarious ne'er-do-wells.

MAKE IT STICK:

Write a few paragraphs in which a crime fighter of your choosing takes on a *nefarious* foe.

HEDONIST
(HEE-duh-nist), noun

One whose life is devoted solely or primarily to the pursuit of pleasure and gratification.

EXAMPLE:

I took offense at Jane's implication that a glass of white wine during dinner made me some kind of **HEDONIST**.

TRIVIA:

The first known use of *hedonist* was in 1806, referring to the Cyrenaics or Kyrenaics, the Greek school of philosophy that essentially believed one should maximize pleasure (usually physical) and minimize pain to achieve personal well-being.

MAKE IT STICK:

If you were to become a *hedonist,* what are three things you wouldn't be able to live without?

1. _____

2. _____

3. _____

VENERATE
(VEN-uh-rate), verb

To regard or treat with the reverence due to one's god/God or holy leader.

EXAMPLE:

"The way the United States **VENERATES** celebrities can be quite annoying," Sylvia said.

TRIVIA:

In George Washington's first inaugural address, he said of his duty to serve, "I was summoned by my Country, whose voice I can never hear but with veneration and love." *Venerate* also applies to people we hold in high regard or who have inspired us.

MAKE IT STICK:

Write a scene using the following: *venerate, Susan, Shannon, Tomb of the Unknown Soldier,* and *wreath.*

_____
_____
_____
_____
_____
_____
_____
_____
_____

JUNKET
(JUNK-it), noun

A recreational trip, outing, or excursion; often, a pleasure trip taken by public officials for the ostensible purpose of gathering facts.

EXAMPLE:

The congressman's eight-week trip to Oahu, supposedly to survey the Hawaiian approach to health care, is only the latest of a long series of **JUNKETS** that call into question his ability to manage public resources with integrity.

TRIVIA:

Junket comes from the fourteenth-century *jonket*, a basket for carrying fish. In the 1520s it became known as a feast or banquet, which might have stemmed from the use of picnic baskets. *Junket* began to mean "pleasure trip" in the early 1800s and, by the late 1800s, it was a pleasure outing made by politicians at taxpayers' expense. But a junket doesn't have to be ill-intentioned. You can take a recreational outing for any reason.

MAKE IT STICK:

Using the word *junket,* describe a recent outing you went on. Where was it? What did you do for fun?

KILTER

(KIL-tur), noun

Working condition; correct position; order.

EXAMPLE:

Although I used a level and ruler when hanging the painting, I could see it was off-**KILTER** when I stepped back to examine it.

TRIVIA:

Although *kilter* showed up in the early 1600s meaning in "good condition" or "working order," today you'll only find *kilter* in the phrases *out of kilter* or *off-kilter*.

MAKE IT STICK:

Write a sentence or short paragraph incorporating the words *kilter*, *washing machine*, and *yoga pants*.

REPARTEE

(reh-per-TEE), noun

Conversation characterized by witty banter.

EXAMPLE:

The **REPARTEE** of the new late-night host seemed rehearsed rather than spontaneous.

TRIVIA:

The skill of witty repartee isn't natural to all of us. As American writer and humorist Mark Twain once said, "Repartee is something we think of twenty-four hours too late."

MAKE IT STICK:

Incorporating *repartee* into your sample, write some witty dialogue between a minister and a soccer coach trying to share a seat on the subway.

BEHEMOTH
(bih-HE-muth), noun

Anything that has monstrous size or power.

EXAMPLE:

What the heck's wrong with Joe? Why did he buy that **BEHEMOTH** gas-guzzler?

TRIVIA:

Behemoth comes from the Hebrew word *b'hemah* or "beast." In the Book of Job in the Old Testament, Behemoth is "a powerful, grass-eating animal whose 'bones are tubes of bronze, his limbs like bars of iron.'" Today, it can also be used figuratively to refer to anything of incalculable size (or frustration!).

MAKE IT STICK:

Finish the scene using *behemoth*: John wrestled with the grill, trying to get it off the back of his pickup truck. It had taken three men to load the grill but, for some reason, he thought he could unload it by himself...

FREEBOOTER
(FREE-boo-ter), noun

A pirate; one who takes his loot—
or booty—without asking.

EXAMPLE:

John quickly thought of Alan as a
FREEBOOTER and not as a
roommate splitting costs fifty-fifty.

TRIVIA:

First used in the 1560s and derived from
the Dutch *vrijbuiter*, meaning "plunderer,
robber," a freebooter is a looter, a term
originally used for pirates. Today the
term can be used to describe people who
steal in settings other than the high seas.

MAKE IT STICK:

What are five ways a person
could be a *freebooter*?

1. _____

2. _____

3. _____

4. _____

5. _____

BOGEY
(BOE-gie), verb, noun

In golf, to post a score of
one stroke over par on a hole;
an instance of such a score.

EXAMPLE:

Jeff **BOGEYED** the fourteenth hole.

TRIVIA:

The word, first coined in 1891, meant the
number of strokes a "good" golf player
should need to complete a given hole
or a particular course. By 1946, it had
shifted to mean scoring one over par.

MAKE IT STICK:

Describe a scene where a golfer *bogeys*
a hole and is furious about it.

_____
_____
_____
_____
_____
_____
_____
_____
_____
_____
_____
_____

KITSCH
(kitch), noun

Something that appeals to lowbrow taste or is overly sentimental, gaudy, and thought indicative of bad taste.

EXAMPLE:

The tourist trap's gift shop was filled with row after row of souvenir **KITSCH**.

MAKE IT STICK:

You're on a beach sojourn and your niece drags you into a gift shop. Using the word *kitsch,* finish the scene.

TRIVIA:

Beauty is in the eye of the beholder, and never has that been more true than in how people choose to decorate their homes or curate sentimental knickknack collections. *Kitsch,* borrowed in the 1920s from the German word of the same spelling, has come to mean trashy, gaudy art or cultural decor. From velvet paintings to porcelain rooster collections to duvet covers printed with "unpopular" art, kitsch abounds. You'll even find plenty of sources for "high-quality lowbrow art" online, so shop away!

TANTALIZE
(TAN-tuhl-ize), verb

To tease or taunt by keeping something desired just out of reach.

EXAMPLE:

Lotteries **TANTALIZE** people with their implied promise of instant wealth. Of course, most people don't win.

TRIVIA:

Tantalos was the mythical king of Phrygia and son of Zeus whose bad deeds caused him anguish in the afterlife. He was made to stand in a lake with boughs of fruit just out of reach. When he tried to get a drink, the water disappeared, and he could never quite reach the fruit to satisfy his hunger.

MAKE IT STICK:

Write a short paragraph using the word *tantalize* about when you were taunted by something you couldn't have.

JUGGERNAUT
(JUG-ur-not), noun

An object or force so powerful
that it flattens or destroys
anything in its path.

EXAMPLE:

The earthquake did some minor struc-
tural damage to the city, but the tor-
nado that followed a week later was
a **JUGGERNAUT**, destroying every
home and building it touched.

TRIVIA:

Juggernaut is a fictional character who
first appeared in Marvel's X-Men comics
in 1965. The character even appeared
in two of the entries in the X-Men film
series in 2006 and 2018.

MAKE IT STICK:

Using the term *juggernaut* figuratively,
write a few sentences describing a work
colleague who is on a path to destroy a
month's worth of work for your team.

BESEECH
(bee-SEECH), verb

To ask for or request **something**
earnestly; to **beg for.**

EXAMPLE:

Jada **BESEECHED** her father to be reasonable and allow her to attend the rally.

TRIVIA:

Beseech originated before 1100 from
the Old English *besecan* and gets a lot of
use in Shakespeare, religious texts, and
highbrow circles requiring something
fancier than *begging*.

MAKE IT STICK:

Write a scene using
beseech, mother, Laura, and *restaurant.*

EXPUNGE

(ex-PUNJ), verb

To do away with utterly; leave no trace.

TRIVIA:

Expunge comes from the Latin word *expungere*, meaning "mark for deletion," and first appeared around 1600. Although we have very few examples of Roman manuscripts, many documents were written on wax tablets. If a word or phrase was to be deleted, the author would underline it with points, using a wooden or ivory stylus.

MAKE IT STICK:

What have you read about recently in the news that humans are trying to *expunge*? Write a short paragraph as if it were an article for a newspaper.

_____

_____

_____

_____

_____

_____

_____

_____

_____

_____

_____

_____

_____

_____

NEANDERTHAL

(knee-AND-er-thall), adjective, noun

Capitalized, *Neanderthal* denotes an early human species whose remains were first discovered in Germany's Neander Valley. With a lowercase *n*, the adjective *neanderthal* is used negatively to describe someone with backward, outdated, old-fashioned attitudes and beliefs.

EXAMPLE:

Of course she was scared away by your **NEANDERTHAL** impulses, Stephen!

TRIVIA:

Neanderthals (with a capital *N*) became extinct 35,000 years ago. There has been a long debate between scientists as to whether or not modern humans replaced other primitive hominins (pre-modern humans) without interbreeding.

MAKE IT STICK:

Using a few sentences, describe a real-life figurative *neanderthal* and compare that person to the imagined traits of a literal *Neanderthal*.

INTERMINABLE
(in-TER-min-uh-bul), adjective

Having or seeming to have no end; wearisomely protracted.

EXAMPLE:
His **INTERMINABLE** questions can become quite annoying.

TRIVIA:
Interminable derives from the Latin roots for "without end." It first appears in the fifteenth century.

MAKE IT STICK:
Write a short scene incorporating the following: *puppy, whine, sleep, Sharron, interminable,* and *night-light.*

_____
_____
_____
_____
_____
_____
_____
_____
_____
_____
_____
_____

INCOGNIZANT
(in-KOG-nih-zant), adjective

Unaware; unintentional; unintended.

EXAMPLE:
Greg was shocked to learn he'd been the **INCOGNIZANT** stooge of a foreign espionage organization.

TRIVIA:
This word first pops up in 1837. Spy novels using characters who are incognizant pawns of foreign powers began appearing in the nineteenth century and reached their zenith in the twentieth century with such authors as John le Carré and Ian Fleming.

MAKE IT STICK:
Write three sentences using *incognizant* in each of its meanings.

1._____
_____

2._____
_____

3._____
_____

MACHIAVELLIAN
(mah-kee-uh-VELL-ee-un), adjective

Cunning and deceitful in the pursuit of power, particularly with regard to political matters; relating to the qualities espoused by Niccolò Machiavelli in his sixteenth-century work, *The Prince*.

EXAMPLE:

Although Lyndon Johnson was certainly a ruthless politician, he was far from the **MACHIAVELLIAN** figure suggested by some of his biographers.

TRIVIA:

In Rodgers and Hammerstein's 1965 musical *The Sound of Music*, Baroness Schraeder confides in her friend Max Detweiler that she intends to send Captain von Trapp's seven children off to boarding school. Max remarks, "Machiavelli."

MAKE IT STICK:

Describe a local political situation where your fictitious mayor is trying to garner more power against the town council by *Machiavellian* means.

JUBILATION

(joo-bih-LAY-shun), noun

An act or expression of extreme joy; a mood of high celebration.

TRIVIA:

Jubilation is an act of celebration or state, whereas a *jubilee* is a special event or celebration, such as the Queen's Jubilee. It is from the late fourteenth-century French meaning "jubilation or rejoicing." It is associated with praise to God in religious sectors and, interestingly, the Spanish word for "retirement" is *jubilación*, a jubilation or celebration for most!

MAKE IT STICK:

Write a journal or diary entry set ten years in the future incorporating the word *jubilation*.

QUAFF
(kwoff), verb

To drink heavily; to engage in the robust intake of alcoholic beverages.

EXAMPLE:

On his twenty-first birthday, Sean vowed he would **QUAFF** at least one glass of beer at every bar in the city.

MAKE IT STICK:

Using the word *quaff*, finish the scene: Ron was a regular at the pub and the bartender, Ralph, slid his usual in front of him...

TRIVIA:

Originally meaning to "overindulge in food and drink," *quaff* now pertains to inhaling one's beverage, usually alcoholic. This merry little report from Thomas D'Urfey's *Wit and Mirth* (circa 1719) makes reference to tavern keeper Simon Wadloe:

For drinking will make a man quaff,
And quaffing will make a man sing;
Singing will make a man laugh,
And laughter long life doth bring.
Says Old Sir Simon the King!

_____
_____
_____
_____
_____
_____
_____
_____
_____
_____
_____
_____
_____
_____
_____
_____
_____
_____
_____
_____
_____

AUSPICIOUS
(aws-PISH-us), adjective

Promising; seemingly favorable or likely to be accompanied by good fortune; usually used to describe encouraging signals or reasons for optimism at the beginning of an undertaking.

EXAMPLE:

The trip did not begin in an **AUSPICIOUS** manner; our car broke down within an hour.

TRIVIA:

Waking to blue skies on your wedding day, being randomly assigned your lucky number for a marathon, or being seated next to England's most eligible bachelor at Wimbledon can all be deemed auspicious. An auspicious occasion refers to a celebratory or momentous event, like a wedding, a presidential inauguration, or a high school or college graduation.

MAKE IT STICK:

Write a scene incorporating *auspicious, provost, graduation, Kristin, Alex,* and *clouds.*

NONPAREIL
(non-puh-RELL), noun

A person without parallel or equal.
Also, a flat chocolate covered with colored sugar.

Frank is hardly the **NONPAREIL** of mystery writing he makes himself out to be.

Write a scene where a child walks into a chocolate shop and purchases dark chocolate *nonpareils*.

TRIVIA:

The candy reference to *nonpareil* originated sometime around the 1690s. They are tiny confectionary balls made with sugar and starch, originally opaque white but available in a myriad of colors beginning in the 1800s. For several hundred years they were used to decorate confections and cakes. In the United States, nonpareils are typically round flat chocolate drops with a coating of tiny round sugar drops.

JOCUND
(JOK-und), adjective

Given to merriment; possessing a cheery disposition.

Tim's **JOCUND** personality made him the life of the party.

Describe a scene using the words *jocund*, *family reunion*, and *Uncle Henning*.

TRIVIA:

In Shakespeare's *Romeo and Juliet*, Romeo uses *jocund* to reference the cheery day that awaits (as long as he leaves Juliet's bedchamber before he's caught!):

It was the lark, the herald of the morn,
No nightingale: look, love, what envious streaks
Do lace the severing clouds in yonder east:
Night's candles are burnt out, and jocund day
Stands tiptoe on the misty mountain tops.
I must be gone and live, or stay and die.

PREDOMINANT
(pree-DAHM-ih-nant), adjective

First or overwhelming in importance; most frequent or common.

TRIVIA:

There's often some confusion between *predominant* and *predominate*. The latter is a verb and adjective, while *predominant* is *only* an adjective. It's also older.

MAKE IT STICK:

Write a short paragraph using *predominant* as something first in importance or most common.

HOMONYM
(HOM-uh-nim), noun

A word that sounds the same as another word, such as *to* and *two*.

TRIVIA:

Homonym is an overarching category that includes homophones and homographs and is used to describe three different categories of words. First, homonyms can be words with identical pronunciations but different spellings and meanings (*to/two/too*). Second, homonyms can be words with the same spellings and pronunciations but have different meanings, such as *bat* (the nocturnal mammal) and *bat* (a baseball bat). Third, homonyms can refer to words spelled the same but pronounced differently, such as *sow* (to plant) or *sow* (a female pig). Some language scholars even limit the use of homonym to words that are spelled the same but pronounced differently. Confusing, indeed! What we can all agree on is that spellcheck will never catch homonym mix-ups, including *pique/peek/peak*, *so/sew/sow*, *to/too/two*, *there/their/they're*, *bear/bare*, *dear/deer*, *tail/tale*, *whine/wine*, and so many more!

MAKE IT STICK:

List *homonyms* in which at least one of the words in each set begins with the following letters:

V _____

_____

_____

W _____

_____

_____

R _____

_____

_____

L _____

_____

_____

P _____

_____

_____

MELEE
(MAY-lay), noun

A confused struggle
involving many people.

EXAMPLE:

After the batter was struck by the pitch-
er's ball, players from both teams ran
out onto the field and a **MELEE** ensued.

TRIVIA:

The English version of this French word
(meaning "meddle") showed up in the
1640s to describe a confused conflict
or a noisy free-for-all, like a bar brawl or
(human) dogfight. The word increased
in notoriety with the arrival of the video
game *Super Smash Bros. Melee* in 2001.

MAKE IT STICK:

Write a sentence or two incorporating
melee, flannel shirt, Jeff, and *Gary*.

_____

_____

_____

_____

_____

_____

_____

_____

WALLOW
(WALL-lo), verb

To utterly immerse oneself;
literally, to roll around in.

EXAMPLE:

Joan's reviews were certainly unflattering
but, in my opinion, she **WALLOWED** in
self-pity after opening night and did the
cast and crew of the show a disservice.

TRIVIA:

The literal meaning "to roll" is from Old
English, and the figurative sense of "to
plunge and remain in some state or condition" is from the early thirteenth century.
Wallowing can be an emotional state, as
in wallowing in sadness, fear, or self-pity,
and it can also be a physical state, as in
literally rolling in mud. Because *wallow* is
often associated with pigs in mud, it has a
negative connotation.

MAKE IT STICK:

Write two sentences using both the figurative and literal meanings of *wallow*.

1. _____

_____

2. _____

_____

REGURGITATE
(rih-GURJ-ih-tate), verb

To vomit; to cast (something) back again.

MAKE IT STICK:

Let's keep this clean, people! Finish this scene using the word *regurgitate*: You're sitting on your front stoop watching a robin bring food back to her nest...

PICAYUNE

(pik-uh-YOON), adjective

Petty; trifling or unimportant.

EXAMPLE:

Mr. Franklin apparently couldn't be bothered with such **PICAYUNE** concerns as what color shirt to wear.

MAKE IT STICK:

Finish the scene using the word *picayune*: Sarah couldn't believe her mom and all her rules, rules, rules…

TRIVIA:

From 1804 and meaning "coin of small value," *picayune* changed quickly to mean "paltry" by 1813. It also refers to small and trivial things. In a murder or accident investigation, it might be the obscure, picayune detail that pieces the mystery together. On the other hand, perhaps not all details are meant to be fussed over. As Amy Vanderbilt, author of the 1952 bestselling book *Amy Vanderbilt's Complete Book of Etiquette*, said, "The best-dressed women I know pay very little attention to the picayune aspects of fashion, but they have a sound understanding of style."

ISTHMUS
(ISS-mus), noun

A narrow strip of land connecting two larger landmasses.

EXAMPLE:

The geologic evidence suggests that, long ago, an **ISTHMUS** linked Siberia and Alaska.

TRIVIA:

The Year Without a Santa Claus, the 1974 stop-motion animated TV special from Rankin/Bass Productions, Mrs. Claus says, "Fast as a hurricane children hurled the happy message around the world. Over each continent, isle, and isthmus, 'Let's give Santa a Merry Christmas.'"

MAKE IT STICK:

Name three *isthmuses*.

1. _____

2. _____

3. _____

DICEY
(DIE-see), adjective

Characterized by being risky, chancy, and of uncertain outcome.

EXAMPLE:

Jordan was filled with confidence about hiking the unexplored terrain but I found the prospect rather **DICEY**.

TRIVIA:

The word originated in the 1940s as aviator jargon. It describes uncertainty, similar to when one rolls a pair of dice. Dicey situations are risky and even dangerous.

MAKE IT STICK:

Finish this scene using *dicey*: Don thought about the fact that he was returning home having sold the Mini without first consulting Ann...

_____

_____

_____

_____

_____

_____

_____

_____

_____

_____

_____

_____

UNALIENABLE

(uhn-AY-lee-un-a-buhl), adjective

Incapable of being taken away.

EXAMPLE:

Although I have always believed freedom of speech to be the **UNALIENABLE** right of every American, I must admit that the diatribes of those who preach hate and violence against members of my race are awfully tough to stomach.

TRIVIA:

The term dates to 1645 but gained its timelessness from the Declaration of Independence: "We hold these truths to be self-evident, that all men are created equal, that they are endowed by their Creator with certain unalienable Rights, that among these are Life, Liberty, and the pursuit of Happiness."

MAKE IT STICK:

Pick one unalienable right. Write a sentence using that right, as well as the word *unalienable*.

NOGGIN
(NOG-in), noun

A small drinking vessel; a mug.

EXAMPLE:

Dinner at our favorite seaport restaurant always began with a generous helping of clam chowder served in old-fashioned ceramic **NOGGINS**.

TRIVIA:

This slang term referring to a "small cup or mug" originated in the early 1600s and morphed to later mean "small drink." The slang use of *noggin* for a person's head came along around the 1860s but no one really knows why. Perhaps, instead of using rolling pins, spouses began hitting each other over the head with their noggins.

MAKE IT STICK:

Incorporating the words *pirate*, *ship*, **noggin**, and *poker*, write a short scene.

VICARIOUS
(vi-KARE-ee-uss), adjective

Arising from the experiences of others rather than one's own.

TRIVIA:

From the 1630s and originally meaning "taking the place of another," many of us live vicariously through the experience of others, but usually in a positive way. Vicarious trauma, however, is something that occurs when you hear about other people having endured terrible things and you "bring their grief, fear, anger, and despair into your own awareness and experience."

MAKE IT STICK:

Write a short paragraph incorporating the following: *vicarious, Venice, Bordeaux, tablecloth,* and *Heather*.

SPECTRE
(SPEK-ter), noun

A ghost or spirit.

EXAMPLE:

As a child, Vern believed a **SPECTRE** lived in his bedroom closet.

TRIVIA:

Although the word first appeared in 1605, it gained popularity in the twentieth century with the comic book character the Spectre, part of the DC Universe, who first appeared in 1940.

MAKE IT STICK:

Describe a scene in which a *spectre* is in your garden or inside your house/apartment. What happens?

SERENITY
(suh-REN-ih-tee), noun

A state of being serene and peaceful;
a lack of agitation.

TRIVIA:

In "The Serenity Now," an episode of
the 1990s sitcom *Seinfeld*, Frank Cos-
tanza learns the phrase from a self-help
tape and puts it to use. Every time he
gets angry and needs to relax in order to
keep his blood pressure down, he blurts
out, "Serenity now!" (which isn't peaceful for anyone nearby!).

MAKE IT STICK:

Describe a time when you experienced
the peace and relaxation of *serenity*.

RABBLE
(RAB-ul), noun

A mob; a rowdy crowd
or disorderly group.

EXAMPLE:

Flashing cameras recorded the journey
of the accused as the police guided him
through the **RABBLE** that had gathered
on the courthouse steps.

TRIVIA:

In the movie *It's a Wonderful Life*,
George Bailey tells the miserly Mr.
Potter that "This rabble you're talking
about, they do most of the working
and paying and living and dying in this
community. Well, is it too much to have
them work and pay and live and die in a
couple of decent rooms and a bath?"

MAKE IT STICK:

Describe a disorderly *rabble* on its way
to a stadium for a baseball game.

RAPACIOUS
(ruh-PAY-shuss), adjective

Given to plunder or the forcible overpowering of another. Related to rape.

MAKE IT STICK:

Test your history. Write a scene from the US Civil War in which there is a *rapacious* character.

TRIVIA:

Coming to English in the 1650s from the Latin words *rapaci* ("grasping") and *rapere* ("to snatch"), it is fittingly used in tales of war and political control. Niccolò Machiavelli, a sixteenth-century Italian Renaissance diplomat regarded as the father of modern political philosophy, said, "War is a profession by which a man cannot live honorably; an employment by which the soldier, if he would reap any profit, is obliged to be false, rapacious, and cruel."

PANDEMONIUM
(pan-duh-MOAN-ee-um), noun

Chaos; wild, uproarious, and noisy tumult.

EXAMPLE:

PANDEMONIUM broke out in the streets of the city after the local team won the pennant.

TRIVIA:

From the seventeenth century, *pandemonium* was coined by poet John Milton in *Paradise Lost* as the name of the great city in Hell.

MAKE IT STICK:

Finish the scene using *pandemonium*:
Cho threw up the window and peered at the street below...

YOKEL
(YOE-kul), noun

A bumpkin; a rustic person.

EXAMPLE:

That one-set show may have impressed the **YOKELS** where you come from, but here in the big city we require a little more flash and stardust from our musicals.

TRIVIA:

In an episode of *The Muppet Show*, the audience boos Gonzo off the stage. Kermit comments, "Looks like it's another wipe-out for Gonzo." Gonzo replies, "Yokels! What do they know about art?"

MAKE IT STICK:

Write a short scene incorporating the following: *yokel, Iowa State Fair, Ferris wheel,* and *livestock barn.*

_____

_____

_____

_____

_____

_____

_____

_____

UNFASTIDIOUS
(un-fass-TID-ee-us), adjective

Harried or in a condition of disarray; unkempt; dirty and limp.

EXAMPLE:

A group of **UNFASTIDIOUS** orphans stood outside begging by the flickering gaslight.

TRIVIA:

This is the negative form of the adjective *fastidious*, which seems to have originated in the fifteenth century. Curiously, back then it meant "squeamishness" or "aversion."

MAKE IT STICK:

Describe a situation in which someone (or an animal) is *unfastidious.*

_____

_____

_____

_____

_____

_____

_____

_____

QUIBBLE
(KWIB-uhl), verb, noun

As a noun, either an instance of using evasive language to avoid the subject at hand *or* an example of petty criticism. As a verb, the act of using evasive language *or* the act of offering petty criticism.

EXAMPLE:

"Do you love me?" Janice asked. Paul **QUIBBLED** for some time, pointing out how much she meant to him and how happy he was with her. Janice knew the answer to her question was no.

TRIVIA:

From the 1610s, *quibble* meant "a pun, a play on words," and might be from the archaic *quib* meaning "evasion of point at issue." *Quibble* is evasive and can also be a small argument or fight. As the late comedian George Carlin said, "I'm certainly a skeptic. I always quibble with people."

MAKE IT STICK:

Finish the scene incorporating the word *quibble*: It was true that Hilary was running very late again, but it wasn't her fault. Ron had infuriated her by staying at the pub an hour longer than promised.

TARANTELLA

(tar-un-TELL-ah), noun

A spirited Italian dance in ⁶⁄₈ time.

EXAMPLE:

Al, a dedicated foxtrotter, had a tough time dealing with his wife's seemingly endless fascination with the **TARANTELLA.**

TRIVIA:

The tarantella is named after the southern Italian town of Taranto. The belief was that the dance was either the result of or cure for the bite of the *tarantola* (*tarantula* in English).

MAKE IT STICK:

Write a scene using *tarantella, Lauren, Jeff, red gown,* and *shoelaces.*

_____
_____
_____
_____
_____
_____
_____
_____

JADED

(JAY-did), adjective

Worn out; dulled or satiated due to overindulgence.

EXAMPLE:

Her parents thought providing Tracy with everything her heart desired as a child would make her a happy person, but she grew up to be a **JADED** and selfish woman.

TRIVIA:

The origins of this word are unclear. In the late 1300s, *jade* meant "an old horse or a cart horse," but by the 1600s it also meant "tired and worn out."

MAKE IT STICK:

Write an acrostic with terms relating to *jaded*:

J _____

A _____

D _____

E _____

D _____

TIRADE
(TIE-raid), noun

An extended outburst of harsh talk; a lengthy, overblown speech.

TRIVIA:

A tirade can be harsh or negative, or it can just be more than the situation warrants. In one scene from the 1982 film *Fast Times at Ridgemont High*, Jeff Spicoli is late to class (as is his wont) and provides an elaborate excuse. His teacher asks, "Why are you continually wasting my time and the class's with this tirade every day?" Spicoli's thoughtful reply is, "Uh, uh...I don't know."

MAKE IT STICK:

Finish this paragraph using the word *tirade*: From a distance, Boyd could hear the customer as he stocked cans of tuna on the shelves. Just then, the customer came around the corner and headed straight for him...

USURP
(yoo-SURP), verb

To assume forcibly and/or without right; to take over.

EXAMPLE:
The authority of Congress was indeed **USURPED** by Lincoln during the war, but legislators briskly reasserted themselves once the crisis was past.

TRIVIA:
When the president of the United States is incapacitated, the vice president assumes responsibility, but when President Ronald Reagan was shot on March 30, 1981, Alexander Haig, Reagan's secretary of state, overstepped his bounds by saying, "I'm in control here..." You can imagine how well that went over.

MAKE IT STICK:
Using the word *usurp,* finish this thought: Sally couldn't say for sure, but she almost thought...

_____

_____

_____

_____

_____

_____

_____

NIGGLING
(NIG-ling), adjective

Petty; annoying.

EXAMPLE:
I could usually deal with my roommate's **NIGGLING** complaints about hairs in the sink and my forgetting to take out the trash, but I was in no mood for it today.

TRIVIA:
In use since the 1590s, the original use of the word meant "to work in a finicky, fussy way." The term morphed to mean "something small and of little importance."

MAKE IT STICK:
Using the word *niggling,* write a few sentences describing an annoying pain or thought you or a loved one has had.

_____

_____

_____

_____

_____

_____

_____

_____

_____

VEXATION
(vek-SAY-shun), noun

Irritation; that which aggravates.

EXAMPLE:

"Where on Earth is my horse?"
Scarlett demanded in **VEXATION**.

TRIVIA:

Vexation has its roots in the Latin *vexa-tionem*, meaning "annoyance, harassing; distress, trouble."

MAKE IT STICK:

Write a short paragraph incorporating *vexation, dog, Pat, basement,* and *John.*

_____

_____

_____

INCOGNITO
(in-cog-NEE-to), adjective

Hidden or unknown;
with one's identity concealed.

EXAMPLE:

The novelist wore sunglasses in hopes of remaining **INCOGNITO** at restaurants, but he was still pestered by autograph hounds.

TRIVIA:

From the 1640s and meaning to be "disguised under an assumed name or character," history and modern times are filled with people trying or needing to travel incognito, from celebrities to spies to Hannah Montana. In J.K. Rowling's Harry Potter series, there are even spells to change one's appearance when necessary.

MAKE IT STICK:

Using the word *incognito,* describe how you'd disguise yourself if you were going to travel incognito.

INDITE
(in-DITE), verb

To cause to come into being by means of artistic effort; to write or compose.

MAKE IT STICK:

Write a sentence or paragraph incorporating *Dave Barry*, **indite**, and *rankle*.

_____
_____
_____
_____
_____
_____
_____
_____
_____
_____

WILE
(wile), noun, verb

As a noun: a clever trick meant to attain a goal; an instance of or talent for beguiling deceit.
As a verb: to lure, entice, or beguile.

MAKE IT STICK:

Write two sentences using *wile*: one as a noun and one as a verb.

1. _____
_____

2. _____
_____

LOCOMOTION

(lo-kuh-MO-shun), noun

The act or ability of moving from place to place.

EXAMPLE:

Children's lack of **LOCOMOTION** today is resulting in an obesity epidemic.

TRIVIA:

When the word originated in the 1640s, it meant "action or power of motion." In 1788 it added the meaning "to move from place to place." Shortly thereafter, *locomotive* was adopted for the name of the rail transport engine powering trains. "The Loco-Motion" is also Little Eva's popular 1962 hit song and dance that made you get up and move from place to place.

MAKE IT STICK:

Finish the scene incorporating *locomotion*: "Shh! Here he comes now!"

JITNEY
(JIT-nee), noun

A small car or bus charging a low fare.

EXAMPLE:

Grandpa told us stories of how he used to make his living driving a **JITNEY** around town.

TRIVIA:

The origins of this word were unknown until 2016, when language scholar Stephen Goranson confirmed that *jitney* was derived from the African-American word *jetnée*, making its way from the French or Creole *jeton*, or "token." The word sounds like something that should have died out decades ago, but jitneys still operate in places like the Hamptons to take you to your beach sojourn.

MAKE IT STICK:

Write a beach scene involving a *jitney*.

HIRSUTE
(HUR-soot), adjective

Hairy.

EXAMPLE:

"Here you are, my **HIRSUTE** friend," Dr. Fredericks called out. "A nice juicy bone from the butcher."

MAKE IT STICK:

Write a few sentences incorporating the words *hirsute, Abominable Snowman,* and *hot chocolate.*

TRIVIA:

Originating from the Latin *hirsutus,* meaning "rough, shaggy, bristly" and sometimes used figuratively to mean "rude and unpolished," *hirsute* gets a lot of traction during the Major League Baseball playoffs when superstitious team members try to outdo each other with the best mountain-man look. Ari Gold, from the HBO comedy-drama *Entourage,* would have had those beards shaved in no time. "Unless you're in an early seventies-era Eagles cover band, a founding member of a religious cult, or sleeping under a bridge in Seattle, lose the beard and get a haircut. Power doesn't have time for any form of hirsute hipster self-expression."

VALIANT
(VAL-ee-unt), adjective

Brave; courageous.

EXAMPLE:

It was the gnome-like Mario, the last person Sergeant Denton would have termed a **VALIANT** young cadet, who ended up winning a medal for risking his own life to save his comrades.

TRIVIA:

Prince Valiant is an American comic strip created by Hal Foster that debuted on February 13, 1937. The strip continues today, although penned by other artists, and has had a run of more than 4,000 Sunday comic pages! Now that's a valiant group effort if ever there was one!

MAKE IT STICK:

Two *valiant* friends are going on an adventure to retrieve a stolen phone from the school bully. What happens?

SCHADENFREUDE
(SHAH-dun-froy-duh), noun

An instance of rejoicing at the misfortune of another.

EXAMPLE:

Wilson's conviction on perjury charges set off a festival of **SCHADENFREUDE** among his many conservative detractors.

TRIVIA:

Naomi Wolf once said of singer and actress Madonna, "Since Madonna is positioned as always 'cooler than thou,' we all are poised for schadenfreude if something in her fabulous life goes amiss."

MAKE IT STICK:

Using today's word, write about a recent time when you saw someone rejoicing in someone else's misfortune.

MARAUD
(muh-ROD), verb

To wander in search of booty; to loot or invade for treasure.

TRIVIA:

Maraud was popularized in several languages during the Thirty Years' War (1618–1648) when people used it tongue in cheek to tell tales of Count Mérode, an imperialist general.

MAKE IT STICK:

Finish the scene using the word *maraud*: Azilee and Eli just wanted to get to the candy cupboard behind their sleeping mother.

JILT

(jilt), verb

To cast (a lover) aside; to discard or dismiss unfeelingly.

EXAMPLE:

After being **JILTED** so abruptly by Michael, Jane found it hard to trust men enough to enter into another relationship.

TRIVIA:

Jilt traces back to the English noun *jillet* which meant "a flirtatious girl." It morphed to mean "an unchaste woman" in the seventeenth century and then "one who casts off a lover." Now both genders can end a romantic relationship, and romance novels abound with titles including the word *jilted*.

MAKE IT STICK:

Write a short scene or paragraph using
jilt, Camaro, Dawn, and *Chunky Monkey ice cream.*

STYMIE
(STIE-mee), verb

To thwart; to prevent (another) from achieving a goal.

MAKE IT STICK:

Write a short scene using the following:
stymie, billboard, Leah, Mike, and *hayfield.*

WOEFUL
(WOH-ful), adjective

Filled with sorrow or woe;
in a sorry state.

EXAMPLE:

When the home team lost the game in the final seconds, the **WOEFUL** crowd gasped and then went silent.

TRIVIA:

From the Hundred Acre Wood comes the most woeful character in all of literature: Eeyore. With his it's-all-for-naught attitude, it's a miracle anyone wants to spend time with him.

MAKE IT STICK:

Finish the scene using *woeful*:
Ray couldn't believe the Capitals
lost another Stanley Cup...

_____

_____

_____

_____

_____

_____

_____

GRAPPLE
(GRAP-ul), verb

To struggle (with an opponent
or enemy); to attempt to pin down
or throw to the ground.

EXAMPLE:

Alert Secret Service agents **GRAPPLED** with the armed intruder and wrestled him to the ground before any shots were fired.

TRIVIA:

This term entered the scene in the 1520s and was a literal reference to wrestling with something, stemming from the noun *grapple*, which was a hook for fastening two things together.

MAKE IT STICK:

Write two sentences: one using *grapple* figuratively and one using it literally.

1. _____

_____

2. _____

_____

EXECRABLE

(EKS-uh-kruh-bull), adjective

Abhorrent; provokes disgust or hatred.

EXAMPLE:

Such **EXECRABLE** sentiments of racial prejudice have no place in this company.

TRIVIA:

From the Latin *execrabilis*, meaning "accursed." Like most Latin-based words, it entered into English by way of Old French. The root of the Latin word is *sacer*, meaning "sacred," so something that was execrable was impious or profane.

MAKE IT STICK:

You or a fictional character of your choosing is next in line to speak at a town meeting. Behind you is a notoriously caustic member of the community. Using the word *execrable,* describe what happens when he/she takes the mic.

HAGGLE
(HAG-ul), verb

To bargain with; to dicker or negotiate on price or terms.

EXAMPLE:

I think Tom enjoyed the process of **HAGGLING** at the flea market more than the items he bought.

TRIVIA:

A Consumer Reports survey notes that nearly half the respondents said they tried to haggle over the price of goods at least once in the past three years, and 89 percent reported they were successful at least once.

MAKE IT STICK:

Write a short paragraph incorporating *haggle*, *scooter*, *Pam*, and *romper*.

MODICUM
(MOD-ih-kuhm), noun

A moderate or token amount.

EXAMPLE:

Darryl always complains about actors who have transformed a **MODICUM** of talent into successful careers.

MAKE IT STICK:

Using the word *modicum*, write about something in which you have a modicum of skill.

TRIVIA:

From the Latin *modicum*, meaning "a little," the English version comes from the Scottish "small quantity or portion" from the late 1400s. The definition now includes "any at all," as in a person having any sense or ounce of courage. Dick Clark, the World's Oldest Teenager, once said of humor that it "is always based on a modicum of truth. Have you ever heard a joke about a father-in-law?" Most of us would agree that family tales generally have a hint of truth to them.

OENOPHILE
(EE-nuh-file), noun

A wine connoisseur.

EXAMPLE:

Len, a lifelong **OENOPHILE**, shuddered as I produced a bottle of Ripple to accompany our dinner of fish sticks and macaroni and cheese.

TRIVIA:

Holless Wilbur Allen, inventor of the compound bow (used in archery), once said, "Books and bottles breed generosity, and the bibliophile and the oenophile og [sic] through life scattering largess from their libraries and cellars."

MAKE IT STICK:

Finish this scene using the word *oenophile*: Dean watched as Brian uncorked the bottle of Tenuta San Guido Sassicaia Bordeaux. He was parched and could almost taste the wine on his lips. "We're just going to let that breathe for a while," Brian said.

GENDARME
(zhon-DARM), noun

An officer in a police force in any of several European countries,
particularly those of France.

EXAMPLE:

After months of difficult undercover
work, the Parisian **GENDARME**
was able to recover the stolen art-
work and return it to its rightful
place in the Louvre.

TRIVIA:

From the 1700s and referring to the
body of soldiers serving to maintain public order, one of the most
famous and beloved gendarmes of all
time is Inspector Clouseau, from the
Pink Panther comic books, cartoons,
and movies.

MAKE IT STICK:

Describe a scene at the Eiffel Tower involving a *gendarme*.

SCINTILLATE
(SIN-til-ate), verb

To give off sparks; to dazzle, impress, or provoke remarkable interest.

EXAMPLE:

News about the new film
has been hard to come by,
but a few leaked details
SCINTILLATED the public.

MAKE IT STICK:

Write a short paragraph incorporating
the words *scintillate*, *candlelight*,
velvet, and *evergreen*.

TRIVIA:

The word comes from the 1620s
from the Latin *scintillatus*, meaning
"to sparkle, glitter, gleam, flash."
Scintillating is the adjective form.
You can enjoy the scintillating stars
in the night sky and scintillating conversation, if it's full of witty repartee
and your conversation partner has
scintillating eyes. Isn't this piece of
trivia scintillating?

DISQUIET
(dis-KWI-et), noun

A misgiving or pang of conscience
(at one's course of action);
anxiety; uneasiness.

EXAMPLE:

He feels **DISQUIET** about
leaving his job; he'd given the company
three very good years.

TRIVIA:

In the 1520s, someone discovered that if
you stuck a *dis* in front of *quiet*, it meant
the opposite, so *disquiet* meant "uneasiness" or, literally, "not peace."

MAKE IT STICK:

Write a short paragraph incorporating
the words *disquiet*, *gunfire*, and *night*.

NATTER
(NA-tuhr), verb

To talk mindlessly and at length.

EXAMPLE:

When the old guy started **NATTERING**,
it made me wish I hadn't stopped
to ask for directions.

TRIVIA:

Natter is from the early 1800s. In the
northern England dialect, *gnatter* meant
"chatter" and "grumble."

MAKE IT STICK:

Using *natter* in a sentence, describe a
scene where a police officer is trying to
hand out a moving violation to a driver
who is nattering on.

ABSOLUTION
(ab-suh-LOO-shun), noun

The condition of having been forgiven or freed of guilt.

TRIVIA:

Originally pertaining to sin, *absolution* became a more general term around 1400. In one of the most somber scenes in the 1997 movie *Titanic*, the elderly Rose describes the mood of the seven hundred survivors who were in lifeboats after the ship sank: "Afterward, the seven hundred people in the boats had nothing to do but wait: wait to die, wait to live, wait for an absolution which would never come."

MAKE IT STICK:

Describe a time or setting in which *absolution* is or is not granted.

OSTRACIZE
(OSS-truh-size), verb

To exclude or banish, as in to exclude someone from a social circle.

EXAMPLE:

Desmond was **OSTRACIZED** from the group after the negative publicity his mother received.

TRIVIA:

Ostracize originally meant "exile" or "banish by popular vote." In ancient Athens, citizens could vote to exile any citizen for ten years. The voting was done by writing the name of the person to be banished on pot shards called *ostraka*.

MAKE IT STICK:

Using the word *ostracize*, describe a recent news event where a member of a group or political party was banished from future activities or participation.

_____

_____

_____

_____

_____

_____

_____

SCHLEMIEL
(shluh-MEEL), noun

An unlucky or awkward individual who never seems to get the best of a situation.

EXAMPLE:

My guess is that the used car salesman had Mike pegged for a **SCHLEMIEL** the second he stepped onto the lot.

TRIVIA:

A Yiddish term meaning "fool." *Happy Days* spin-off *Laverne & Shirley*'s opening credits sequence gave *schlemiel* (and *schlimazel!*) some extra press.

MAKE IT STICK:

Write one or two sentences incorporating the words *schlemiel*, *horse track*, and *bookie*.

_____

_____

_____

_____

_____

_____

_____

HARANGUE
(huh-RANG), verb, noun

To lecture or berate; an instance of such berating.

EXAMPLE:

Professor Thomas kept me after class to **HARANGUE** me for handing in a handwritten term paper.

TRIVIA:

Originally referring to any speech to a public assembly, the term turned to meaning "a rant," perhaps in part because many public speakers appeared bombastic and agitated when they delivered their speeches with passion. You can harangue or be on the receiving end of a harangue.

MAKE IT STICK:

Finish the scene using *harangue*: Meredith realized she would have to explain that her mother's car broke down before she made it to work. She dialed her mother's number and waited for her to answer...

ROTUNDA

(roh-TUN-duh), noun

A small vending booth built on a circular plan.

EXAMPLE:

Once out of the subway station, I picked up a copy of *The New York Times* at a **ROTUNDA**.

TRIVIA:

Rotundas, though often referring to circular vending booths, can also refer to any building with a circular building plan. The Jefferson Memorial in Washington, DC, for instance, is a rotunda, and the area beneath the Capitol Building's dome is referred to as *the rotunda*.

MAKE IT STICK:

What are five things sold at mall *rotundas*?

1. _____

2. _____

3. _____

4. _____

5. _____

NEPOTISM

(NEP-uh-tiz-um), noun

The practice of favoring relatives.

EXAMPLE:

The company practiced shameless **NEPOTISM**, regularly passing up qualified applicants and hiring the underqualified sons, daughters, and cousins of board members.

TRIVIA:

Nepotism comes from the Latin *nepotem*, meaning "grandson or nephew."

MAKE IT STICK:

Have you ever worked in a situation where family members were given jobs or special treatment? Using the word *nepotism*, describe one situation in which the favored family member didn't live up to expectations.

_____

_____

_____

_____

_____

_____

_____

_____

_____

PHLEGMATIC
(fleg-MAT-ic), adjective

Having a calm, unexcitable temperament.

EXAMPLE:

Allan's **PHLEGMATIC** personality was certainly helpful in keeping us all from panicking during the deadline crunch.

TRIVIA:

Phlegmatic came to English in the fourteenth century, loosely meaning "calm, cool, and collected." In the 1960 film *Spartacus*, Gracchus says, "You and I have a tendency towards corpulence. Corpulence makes a man reasonable, pleasant, and phlegmatic."

MAKE IT STICK:

Finish the scene using *phlegmatic*: Brendan's mother screamed and stomped her feet. "Somebody needs to get that snake out of here right now!"

MOIL

(moyl), noun, verb

Hard, grinding work; to engage in such work.

EXAMPLE:

The **MOIL** of paperwork made Sheila long for early retirement.

TRIVIA:

Moil derives from the Latin *mollis*, meaning "soft," and the Old French *moillier*, meaning "to wet, moisten." The "hard work" interpretation of the word seems to come from the combination of "toil and moil," with *moil* now referring to work that is drudgery.

MAKE IT STICK:

Create a detailed scene using a character of your choosing in which he/she must tackle a boatload of work. Be sure to use *moil*!

UNWONTED
(un-WAHNT-id), adjective

Not typical, habitual, or ordinary.

EXAMPLE:

January's **UNWONTED** warm weather was far from unwanted!

TRIVIA:

As the example suggests, unwonted things aren't necessarily unwanted, but they *are* atypical. As author George Eliot said, "Unwonted circumstances may make us all rather unlike ourselves: there are conditions under which the most majestic person is obliged to sneeze, and our emotions are liable to be acted on in the same incongruous manner."

MAKE IT STICK:

Write a sentence or two incorporating the following: *unwonted, fair, cotton candy, Emily,* and *Paige.*

FALLOW
(FAL-low), adjective

Describing land: uncultivated; plowed but not seeded for a season or more in order to improve the soil. Not active or in use.

EXAMPLE:

Brenda's creative forces have been **FALLOW** since she completed her third novel.

TRIVIA:

Fallow land means a crop isn't grown in the field in order for the soil to rest and rejuvenate minerals. This sustainable land management practice has been used for centuries.

MAKE IT STICK:

Resting might feel like a waste of time, but it's critical for higher yield and productivity. Can you think of a time when being *fallow* unlocked your creativity? Jot down your thoughts.

XENOPHOBE
(ZEE-nuh-fobe), noun

One who fears anything foreign or different; one who regards people, places, or customs that differ from one's own as inherently dangerous.

EXAMPLE:

I don't believe my opponent is really a **XENOPHOBE**, despite his rhetoric against foreigners; he is simply a canny, wealthy, and extremely dangerous demagogue.

TRIVIA:

It's probably not a coincidence that this term was coined at the turn of the last century. Thanks to the industrial revolution and urbanization that began in the 1880s, the United States faced a new wave of immigration, with twenty million immigrants arriving over forty years.

MAKE IT STICK:

Write a scene using *xenophobe*, *rice noodles*, *skeptical*, and *Auntie Ruth*.

NIMBUS

(NIM-bus), noun

A halo-like source of light above the head of a saint or spiritual figure.

EXAMPLE:

The mosaic depicts Christ and his disciples with bright **NIMBUSES**.

TRIVIA:

The word originates from the Latin *nimbus*, meaning "cloud," and possibly *nebula*, meaning "cloud, mist." Perhaps the idea of being up in the clouds is why author J.K. Rowling chose the name Nimbus 2000 for Harry Potter's Quidditch broom.

MAKE IT STICK:

Describe a scene in which your not-so-angelic character enters a room where his/her *nimbus* can be seen by others.

_____

_____

_____

_____

_____

_____

_____

_____

_____

_____

_____

_____

SOLILOQUY

(suh-LIL-uh-kwee), noun

In drama, a speech given by a character as if no one else is present on stage; can also be any discourse a person gives to himself/herself, or an account of a person's inner thoughts.

EXAMPLE:

Hamlet's third act **SOLILOQUY** was delivered in a strange, choppy manner I found most unsettling.

TRIVIA:

Some confuse soliloquy and monologue. A monologue is a tedious speech made by one person in a conversation, such as your Aunt Edna who won't let you get a word in edgewise. A soliloquy is when a character on stage speaks his/her thoughts out loud to the audience but the other characters can't hear it.

MAKE IT STICK:

From a current novel you're reading or TV show you're watching, write a scene in which your favorite character delivers a *soliloquy*.

VACILLATING
(VAA-sih-lay-ting), adjective

Uncertain or undecided.

EXAMPLE:
Jasmine is always so **VACILLATING** when we ask her to come out for drinks.

TRIVIA:
This word entered the language in the 1590s and comes from the Latin *vacillāre*, meaning "to sway to and fro." By the 1620s it had come to mean "waver between two opinions."

MAKE IT STICK:
List three things, from foods to sporting events to TV shows, about which you are *vacillating*.

1. _____

2. _____

3. _____

NOUGAT
(NOO-gut), noun

A type of candy containing nuts and honey.

EXAMPLE:
The new candy bar contained an appealing mixture of **NOUGAT**, caramel, and milk chocolate.

TRIVIA:
Originally from the French meaning "sweetmeat made from almonds and other nuts," today nougat runs the gamut from stiff, chewy, teeth-sticking filling (think Snickers) to light and airy (like a 3 Musketeers bar).

MAKE IT STICK:
Invent your own chocolate bar with a *nougat* filling and write a marketing sales pitch!

_____

_____

_____

_____

_____

_____

_____

_____

CHINTZY
(CHINT-see), adjective

Considered cheap,
tacky, or of low quality.

EXAMPLE:

Angela insisted on wearing a **CHINTZY** leopard-skin jumpsuit and high heels to the company Christmas party.

TRIVIA:

Novelist George Eliot (*The Mill on the Floss, Silas Marner*) is attributed with coining the term *chintzy*. She wrote to her sister in 1851 describing an inferior fabric, apparently a cheap British imitation of real chintz (a cloth decorated with Indian-derived designs).

MAKE IT STICK:

Write about a purchase in which you received something cheap or tacky. Use *chintzy* to describe it.

_____

_____

_____

_____

_____

_____

ZENITH
(ZEE-nith), noun

The highest point attained; the apex of something.

EXAMPLE:

Sandy Koufax's baseball career reached its **ZENITH** in 1963 when he won twenty-five games and was unanimously awarded the Cy Young Award.

TRIVIA:

From the late fourteenth century and originally meaning "the point of the heavens directly overhead at any place," it's an astronomical term describing the highest point in the sky reached by a planet, star, or other heavenly body.

MAKE IT STICK:

Write two sentences using *zenith*— one from the point of view of a hiker and another describing an accomplishment.

1._____

_____

_____

2._____

_____

_____

RAMBUNCTIOUS
(ram-BUNK-shuss), adjective

Difficult to manage or control; extremely boisterous.

TRIVIA:

In *Batman: Mystery of the Batwoman*, Bruce Wayne encounters Oswald Cobblepot (a.k.a. The Penguin). Bruce comments that the last time they saw each other was when Oswald stole plutonium from one of Bruce's labs and threatened to blow up the city. "Oh, oh yes," Oswald responded. "My more rambunctious days."

MAKE IT STICK:

Finish the scene using the word *rambunctious*: Jack and Tyler tore through the living room, tripping over the area rug and crashing into the coffee table…

LEVITY

(LEH-vih-tee), noun

Lightness; insubstantiality;
excessive or unseemly frivolity.

EXAMPLE:

Gentlemen, with all due respect, we face a crisis; this is no time for **LEVITY**.

TRIVIA:

Levity (as in "devoid of seriousness") dates to the 1560s. It was picked up in the 1600s by the scientific community and thought to be a force opposite of gravity (for example, when a helium balloon rises).

MAKE IT STICK:

Fill out this acrostic with adjectives related to *levity*:

L _____

E _____

V _____

I _____

T _____

Y _____

_____

NADIR

(NAY-dur), noun

Lowest point.

EXAMPLE:

The **NADIR** of my writing career was probably that spell in Omaha when I wrote obituaries for the local newspaper.

TRIVIA:

Used during its first 400 years in the English language in a purely astronomical sense ("opposite to the zenith of the sun" or "inferior pole of the horizon"), its use as "lowest point" joined our vernacular in 1793.

MAKE IT STICK:

Think of a beloved cartoon character. Describe the character's *nadir*.

_____

_____

_____

_____

_____

_____

_____

ORNERY

(ORE-nuh-ree), adjective

Stubborn or unyielding; inclined toward obstinate behavior.

EXAMPLE:

Grandma insists Grandpa was an easygoing fellow in his youth, but since their move from the country he's become quite **ORNERY**.

TRIVIA:

Some notable ornery characters are Ron Swanson (*Parks and Recreation*), Red Forman (*That '70s Show*), Jay Pritchett (*Modern Family*), Oscar the Grouch (*Sesame Street*), Roz (*Monsters, Inc.*), and Ove Lindahl (*A Man Called Ove*).

MAKE IT STICK:

Using *ornery*, flesh out this short scene: You're in the grocery store and overhear an elderly man shouting at an employee because he can't find the brand of butter he wants.

WIZENED
(WIZ-und), adjective

Old; shriveled.

TRIVIA:

Not to be confused with *wise* or *wisenheimer*, although someone who comments to their dear Aunt Martha "You're looking a little wizened today" might be called a wisenheimer!

MAKE IT STICK:

Write a humorous scene from a Christmas dinner incorporating the following: *wizened*, Lois, *coconut pie*, and *coffeepot*.

UPSIDE
(UP-side), noun

The positive aspect of a situation; particularly,
the potential profit in a business proposal.

EXAMPLE:

The **UPSIDE** of investing in the Russian company was considerable, but there were considerable risks as well.

TRIVIA:

Originally meaning "upper side," the term morphed to mean "the positive facet of a situation" by 1927. In 1970, *upside one's head* referenced taking a blow to the head.

MAKE IT STICK:

Write a short scene incorporating *upside, Laurel, frog,* and *science project.*

WANTON

(WON-tun), adjective

Completely unrestrained;
done without justification.

EXAMPLE:

Such **WANTON**, pointless cruelty, even
in the name of science, is inexcusable.

TRIVIA:

Wanton came to English in the mid-
fifteenth century and was made popular
in Shakespeare's writings.

MAKE IT STICK:

Write two sentences using the
two definitions of *wanton*.

1. _____
   _____
   _____

2. _____
   _____
   _____

FLIMFLAM

(FLIM-flam), noun

A swindle; a scam
or confidence game.

EXAMPLE:

Vern may call himself an entrepreneur,
but it appears to me he's nothing more
than a **FLIMFLAM** artist.

TRIVIA:

The Flim-Flam Man, starring George
C. Scott, featured a rural con artist
who travels through small towns in the
American south cheating the locals out
of their money through card tricks and
other similar schemes.

MAKE IT STICK:

Describe a *flimflam* operation that
might have taken place in the 1920s.

_____
_____
_____
_____
_____
_____
_____
_____
_____

ZEITGEIST
(TSIGHT-giced), noun

The taste and outlook—the "spirit"—common to a particular age.

EXAMPLE:

That band has survived for decades because it always seems to make an accurate assessment of the current **ZEITGEIST**.

TRIVIA:

From 1848 and the German *zeitgeist* ("spirit of the age"), iconic elements of various periods are referred to as *zeitgeists*. Flappers and speakeasies were the spirit of the 1920s, hippies and Woodstock marked the 1960s, and leg warmers, boom boxes, and big hair were icons of the 1980s. Early twenty-first-century zeitgeists would likely include mobile phones and political distrust.

MAKE IT STICK:

If you had to fill a time capsule with the *zeitgeist* of today, what would you put in it?

_____
_____
_____
_____
_____
_____
_____

MARZIPAN
(MAR-zuh-pan), noun

A popular candy made from almonds, egg whites, and sugar.

EXAMPLE:

In Europe, it's quite common to decorate a Christmas tree with edible decorations, including gingerbread men, **MARZIPAN** animals, and miniature fruitcakes.

TRIVIA:

In the Middle Ages, physicians sold marzipan for the treatment of physical and mental disorders, and it's been popular in art and literature from the Brothers Grimm to Tchaikovsky's ballet *The Nutcracker*. January 12 is National Marzipan Day, but in Europe it should probably be December 25, as marzipan is the traditional icing for Christmas cakes.

MAKE IT STICK:

Describe a fictional land of cotton candy and chocolate pudding waterfalls. Be sure to include *marzipan*!

_____
_____
_____
_____
_____
_____
_____

GLISSANDO
(glih-SAHN-doe), noun

In music, a rapid and continuous transition between intervals, such as the sound a slide trombone or pedal steel guitar makes in moving from one note to another.

EXAMPLE:

Since there's no way to "bend" its notes, the piano cannot produce a true **GLISSANDO.**

TRIVIA:

The first known use of the term was in 1854. Perhaps the most prominent glissando in all of classical music is the famed clarinet introduction to George Gershwin's "Rhapsody in Blue."

MAKE IT STICK:

Finish this sentence using the word *glissando*:
The oboist sat poised on the edge of her seat...

VIRTUOSO

(vur-choo-OWE-so), noun

A supremely skilled artist.

TRIVIA:

From the 1610s, meaning "scholar, connoisseur." You can be a virtuoso in areas other than the arts. Athletes, business gurus, and politicians can all be virtuosos.

MAKE IT STICK:

Finish this scene incorporating *virtuoso*: John and Kay spread out their blanket on the Tanglewood lawn, waiting for the Pops concert to begin.

TIMBRE
(TAM-bur), noun

A quality of sound, usually musical, determined by its overtones;
a distinctive quality or tone.

EXAMPLE:

I feel that the haunting **TIMBRE** of the oboe, when played by a master, is more moving than that of any other musical instrument.

TRIVIA:

Timbre and tone are similar but refer to two different attributes of sound. While timbre refers to how sound differs between instruments (such as guitar versus violin), tone refers to how sound can differ on the same instrument (bass versus treble).

MAKE IT STICK:

Write a scene set in the first balcony of a symphony hall incorporating the following: *timbre, Brendan, trumpet,* and *Mahler No. 5.*

WUNDERKIND
(VOON-dur-kind), noun

Child prodigy.

EXAMPLE:

Although he died young, Mozart, a **WUNDERKIND** whose career in music began at the age of six, had a career that spanned two and a half decades.

TRIVIA:

From the German *wunderkind*, literally "wonder-child," this term was first used in English in 1883 and is especially used in reference to musical prodigies but can cover any area of expertise and skill. History is dotted with wunderkinds, including Wolfgang Amadeus Mozart (composer), Pablo Picasso (painter), Blaise Pascal (mathematician), and Clara Schumann (pianist).

MAKE IT STICK:

Incorporating the word *wunderkind,* write about a child prodigy you find fascinating.

_____
_____
_____
_____
_____
_____
_____

CACOPHONY
(kuh-KAHF-uh-knee), noun

Harsh, unpleasant sounds that can create a disturbing feeling.

EXAMPLE:

The **CACOPHONY** of the nearby construction site made it almost impossible to get any work done.

TRIVIA:

Poets will sometimes use cacophony for dramatic effect in their works. One of the most famous uses of *cacophony* is in Edgar Allan Poe's "The Raven," which uses cacophonous-sounding words to call to mind the sounds a raven makes.

MAKE IT STICK:

Describe four different *cacophonies.*

1._____
_____

2._____
_____

3._____
_____

4._____
_____

INFERNAL
(in-FER-nul), adjective

Fiendish; devilish; of or pertaining to hell.
Often used as a mild expletive.

EXAMPLE:

This **INFERNAL** copier keeps breaking down!

TRIVIA:

From the late fourteenth century and referring to the underworld, *infernal* is often used today in conjunction with *racket*.

MAKE IT STICK:

Finish the scene using *infernal*: She woke to a gathering of crows outside her bedroom window. She glanced at the clock.

MANDOLIN

(man-duh-LINN), noun

An eight-stringed fretted instrument similar to a lute.

EXAMPLE:

Patrick called the **MANDOLIN** player over to serenade the table while he asked Jeannie for her hand in marriage.

TRIVIA:

Used originally for folk music, this instrument has been used in recent years by pop and rock musicians such as Led Zeppelin ("The Battle of Evermore," "Going to California"), Styx ("Boat on the River"), Rod Stewart ("Maggie May"), Bruce Hornsby and the Range ("Mandolin Rain"), and even the band from the cult film of the same name, Spinal Tap ("Stonehenge").

MAKE IT STICK:

Finish the scene using *mandolin*: The band showed up at the nightclub packed full of men wearing Harley-Davidson T-shirts.

RIFF
(riff), noun

In music, especially jazz and rock, a short melodic phrase repeated as background or used as a main theme.

EXAMPLE:

Once the bass player started playing the insistent opening **RIFF** to "My Girl," people poured out onto the dance floor.

TRIVIA:

Riffs are short, recognizable musical phrases that would be easily guessed on a *Name That Tune* remake. Riffs can be vocal (The Tokens' "The Lion Sleeps Tonight") or instrumental (the piano in Carole King's "I Feel the Earth Move," the guitar openings of The Beatles' "Day Tripper," and Guns N' Roses' "Sweet Child o' Mine").

MAKE IT STICK:

Finish this scene incorporating *riff*: Amy and Eric sat in a dimly lit jazz club waiting for the trio to start playing. When they finally came out, they began with an iconic jazz chart...

YAMMER

(YAM-mer), verb

To complain loudly; to whine.

EXAMPLE:

While Diane was **YAMMERING** about how hard it was to get the office plants watered properly, I was trying to meet a deadline.

TRIVIA:

From the fifteenth century and meaning "to lament," *yammering* is something that grates on the nerves of others.

MAKE IT STICK:

Using the word *yammer*, describe a scene where one of your coworkers is ranting about employee-of-the-month parking spaces.

BEATIFIC
(bee-uh-TIFF-ic), adjective

Having a saintly or angelic character or demeanor.

EXAMPLE:

Charlie's **BEATIFIC** smile always makes me wonder what he's thinking.

TRIVIA:

From the 1630s and meaning "blissful, imparting bliss," *beatific* often refers to a genuine smile, one that conveys a peaceful sense of joy. *Beatific* can be used to describe anything in a state of bliss.

MAKE IT STICK:

Write a short scene from a shopping excursion that incorporates *beatific, sigh, cheesecake,* and *gift.*

TROUBADOUR

(TROO-buh-dore), noun

A traveling medieval poet and singer; any wandering singer or minstrel.

EXAMPLE:

After college, Ivan fancied himself something of a **TROUBADOUR** and wandered from town to town in search of coffeehouses willing to let him play.

TRIVIA:

Although troubadours are generally thought of as being from medieval times, the term is still used to refer to some current poets/musicians. In fact, the Troubadour, a popular nightclub in West Hollywood, made *Rolling Stone*'s list of Best Clubs in America.

MAKE IT STICK:

Write a short scene or paragraph incorporating the following: *Jim, Becky, campground, troubadour,* and *guitar.*

DUDGEON
(DUD-jee-un), noun

Intense ill will; bitter resentment.

EXAMPLE:

Mike's **DUDGEON** toward his ex-wife was so intense that the mere mention of her was sometimes enough to send him into a tirade.

TRIVIA:

Dudgeon derives from the Middle English *dogeon* and from the 1570s *duggin*, meaning a "feeling of offense, resentment, sullen anger." *Dudgeon* was also a dagger handle, referenced in Shakespeare's writings, among other places.

MAKE IT STICK:

Have you or a friend ever experienced intense *dudgeon*? Describe it.

_____

_____

_____

_____

_____

_____

_____

_____

_____

PREROGATIVE
(puh-ROGG-uh-tive), noun

A right or privilege limited to a particular person in a particular situation.

EXAMPLE:

The manager exercised his **PREROGATIVE** to stop the bickering during the staff meeting.

TRIVIA:

In the sitcom *Parks and Recreation*, Ron Swanson tries to teach a fourth grader about taxes using her lunch as a metaphor. "If you want to eat all of it, great. If you want to throw it away, that's your prerogative." He takes a bite of her sandwich. When she protests, Ron says, "You're learning. Uh-oh! Capital gains tax!" and takes another bite.

MAKE IT STICK:

Incorporating today's word, write about a time when you had a *prerogative*.

_____

_____

_____

_____

_____

_____

_____

SLOVENLY
(SLUHV-in-lee), adjective

Dirty or untidy in one's personal habits.

EXAMPLE:

Burt's **SLOVENLY** room is at odds with his tidy personal appearance.

TRIVIA:

Classic film slobs abound, from Oscar Madison (*The Odd Couple*) and Jeffrey "The Dude" Lebowski (*The Big Lebowski*) to Floyd (*True Romance*) and Carl Spackler (*Caddyshack*).

MAKE IT STICK:

Write a short scene including the words *slovenly*, *ironing board*, *sink*, and *sofa*.

OPUS
(OPE-us), noun

A major work (of art or literature).
In English, *opuses* is the accepted plural.

EXAMPLE:

Although he had been working on it for over a year and a half, the composer was less than halfway done with his **OPUS**.

TRIVIA:

Usually musical in nature, an opus is a significant piece of work. *Opera* is derived from a plural form of *opus*. The term *magnum opus* refers to one's greatest work, musical or otherwise. While this sort of thing is subjective, some examples might be Richard Wagner's *Der Ring des Nibelungen*, Mozart's *The Marriage of Figaro*, and, as Charlotte the spider said in E.B. White's *Charlotte's Web*, her egg sack.

MAKE IT STICK:

Using the word *opus*, talk about a person's major accomplishment.

PERSIFLAGE
(PUR-sih-flajh), noun

A humorous use of sarcasm or irony in order to ridicule, expose, or make light of a person, institution, or practice; light banter.

EXAMPLE:

I was merely using **PERSIFLAGE** when I said Aunt Becky's cookies could be weaponized and shot from howitzers.

TRIVIA:

From the French *persifler*, meaning "to banter," and the Latin *sibilare*, with a similar meaning. This word isn't used much anymore, which is rather sad for most of us, except maybe Aunt Becky.

MAKE IT STICK:

What is your favorite bit of persiflage in a movie?
Write a completely new scene with those characters, still using *persiflage*.

OPULENT

(OP-yoo-lent), adjective

Rich; characterized by wealth or affluence,
such as an extravagant dinner party.

EXAMPLE:

Without the money from Powers,
Hans knew he'd be unable to maintain his **OPULENT** lifestyle.

TRIVIA:

Opulence is best summed up in the
accounts of the gross materialism
of the Gilded Age, the luxury of the
Titanic, F. Scott Fitzgerald's 1925
novel *The Great Gatsby*, and by taking a walk along Newport, Rhode
Island's Cliff Walk, where each man-
sion tries to outdo the next.

MAKE IT STICK:

Using the words *opulent*, *crystal*, and *cashmere*,
describe a party scene you observe by peering over a fence.

_____

_____

_____

_____

_____

_____

_____

_____

_____

_____

_____

_____

_____

_____

_____

URBANE

(ur-BANE), adjective

Suave; sophisticated; debonair.

EXAMPLE:

Clive, Linda's **URBANE** English cousin, was pleasant company for all of us during his stay here.

TRIVIA:

Miguel de Unamuno, the Spanish essayist and novelist whose writing themes include the need to preserve one's personal integrity when challenged with the issues of conformity, fanaticism, and hypocrisy, once said, "Every peasant has a lawyer inside of him, just as every lawyer, no matter how urbane he may be, carries a peasant within himself."

MAKE IT STICK:

Write a few sentences or a short paragraph incorporating the following: *cottage, Mary Anne, **urbane**,* and *hydrangeas.*

TUTELAGE
(TOOT-l-ij), noun

The act of providing guided instruction or protection; close instruction.

EXAMPLE:

It was under Dr. Clay's **TUTELAGE** that he came to understand how much craft was required to write a solid play.

TRIVIA:

In the 1987 film *Beverly Hills Cop II*, the mayor of Beverly Hills, in an effort to get detective Axel Foley out of trouble with his boss, tells Foley's boss that the detective claims to have "acquired all his skills under *your* expert tutelage."

MAKE IT STICK:

Write a sentence or two using the following: *art gallery*, *tutelage*, *Andy*, and *apprentice*.

_____

_____

_____

_____

_____

_____

_____

DILETTANTE
(DIL-uh-tont), noun

Someone with only an amateurish or aimless interest in a subject or discipline, such as a person who cultivates a superficial knowledge of modern art solely to impress others.

EXAMPLE:

The cafe was once a meeting place for struggling artists and poets of genuine talent but is now nothing more than a swamp of **DILETTANTES**.

TRIVIA:

The word *dilettante* comes from the Latin *delectare*, meaning "to find delight in." It originally referred to someone who enjoyed an array of interests and was considered a positive attribute.

MAKE IT STICK:

What are three areas in which you consider yourself a *dilettante*?

1. _____

2. _____

3. _____

CRYPTIC
(KRIP-tik), adjective

Strange; mysterious or otherworldly; terse and uncommunicative.

EXAMPLE:

Greg was extraordinarily **CRYPTIC** during dinner, even for him.

TRIVIA:

Cryptic comes from the Greek word *kryptein*, meaning "to hide." Unsurprisingly, it's related to the word *crypt*, "a tomb," and *apocrypha*, referring to writings outside an established canon. We also have words like *cryptography*, meaning "the study of secret writing."

MAKE IT STICK:

Write a scene incorporating *cryptic, Maya,* and *code.*

PLETHORA

(PLETH-er-uh), noun

Excessive oversupply.

EXAMPLE:

The new edition contains
a **PLETHORA** of trivia concerning
the films made by Mr. Howard and his
cohorts in the forties and fifties.

TRIVIA:

In the 1986 film *Three Amigos!*, Jefe
says he has many piñatas for El Guapo.
El Guapo asks, "Would you say I have a
plethora of piñatas?"

MAKE IT STICK:

Using *plethora,* describe a scene
in which there is an oversupply of
something you really dislike!

RELINQUISH

(ri-LING-kwish), verb

To give up; to surrender
or forswear something.

EXAMPLE:

The king **RELINQUISHED** his throne
in order to marry the woman he loved.

TRIVIA:

From the mid-fifteenth century and
meaning "desert, abandon." You can
physically relinquish things (like toddlers
releasing coveted toys from their grip)
or figuratively relinquish control of a
group or the idea of sticking with a plan.

MAKE IT STICK:

Describe a time you had to *relinquish*
something very precious to you.

VENDETTA

(ven-DET-uh), noun

A bitter feud or grudge.

EXAMPLE:

Mark's arguments against my proposed project had less to do with its merits than with the **VENDETTA** he's held against me since I was hired for the job he wanted.

TRIVIA:

The word has its origins from the Latin *vindicta*, meaning "vengeance or revenge." Some of the more famous vendettas in history include the Blues and the Greens during the Byzantine Empire, the Hatfields and the McCoys, Joseph Stalin and Leon Trotsky, and Al Capone and Bugs Moran.

MAKE IT STICK:

Make up a fictitious feud using the following:
vendetta, barbecue pit, cologne, and *Fourth of July.*

WHIMSICAL
(WIM-zih-kul), adjective

Fanciful; given to acting on sudden notions or ideas.

EXAMPLE:

Maurice is known as a real sourpuss around the office, but as his college roommate I can tell you he does have his **WHIMSICAL** side.

TRIVIA:

While fanciful and given to sudden notions and ideas (or whims!), *whimsical* can also mean "odd." Whimsical characters in literature include Luna Lovegood from the Harry Potter series (odd) and Alice from *Alice's Adventures in Wonderland* (acting on sudden ideas or whims).

MAKE IT STICK:

Finish the scene incorporating the word *whimsical*:
Shirley stared at the nursery her mother had decorated for the baby.

WISEACRE

(WIZE-ake-ur), noun

A know-it-all; one who professes to know everything.

EXAMPLE:

"Listen, you little **WISEACRE!**" Sergeant Artemis howled at Corporal Budworth. "If you think you can train these recruits better than I can, you ought to try it sometime!"

TRIVIA:

From the Middle Dutch *wijssegger* meaning "soothsayer," *wiseacre* entered the English vernacular in the 1590s and means "a smart aleck or wisenheimer."

MAKE IT STICK:

Write a scene using the following:
Samantha, **wiseacre,** *Derek, fishing pole,* and *bait.*

UTOPIA
(yoo-TOE-pee-uh), noun

A (theoretical) perfect society or paradise.

EXAMPLE:

Any notion that granting eighteen-year-olds the right to vote would turn the country into a pastoral, strife-free **UTOPIA** was quickly disproven.

TRIVIA:

Coined by using Greek forms to produce a word meaning "nowhere." Sixteenth-century author (and saint) Thomas More coined the term in a book describing an imaginary island where all political, legal, and social systems were perfect and operated without incident. The 2016 animated feature film *Zootopia* was a spoof on utopia but also showed that what they hoped would be a perfect society didn't exist when all was said and done.

MAKE IT STICK:

What would a utopian world (or house!) look like for you? Describe it, being sure to use *utopia*!

_____
_____
_____
_____
_____
_____
_____
_____
_____
_____
_____
_____
_____
_____
_____
_____
_____
_____
_____
_____
_____

NIRVANA

(nir-VAW-nuh), noun

**A point or state of spiritual perfection;
a transcendent state beyond the concerns of existence.**

EXAMPLE:

Some of the monks have meditated and maintained complete silence for years in an attempt to achieve **NIRVANA**.

TRIVIA:

The band Nirvana, popular in the early 1990s, went by several other names originally, such as Skid Row. According to band member Kurt Cobain, they changed their name because they "wanted a name that was kind of beautiful or nice and pretty instead of a mean, raunchy punk name like the Angry Samoans."

MAKE IT STICK:

Describe a scene where a character (real or imagined) is striving for *nirvana* but can't quite attain it.

MACABRE

(ma-KAH-bra), adjective

Having weird, uncanny, or exotic features.

EXAMPLE:

I wouldn't call Jim **MACABRE**, but his favorite activities are touring local cemeteries and taking pictures of area funeral homes.

TRIVIA:

The word pops up in the early fifteenth century in *The Danse Macabre*, a morality play to persuade watchers to shun evil and embrace good. The origin is certainly French and by the nineteenth century it had come to mean "associated with gruesome."

MAKE IT STICK:

Describe a *macabre* house decorated for Halloween.

PIQUANCY

(PEE-kwan-see), noun

The state of being provocative and mentally exciting; a sharp, spicy quality.

EXAMPLE:

Annabel's desire to add **PIQUANCY** to her life led her enthusiastically into modern dance, mountain climbing, and untold hours of volunteer work.

TRIVIA:

In Middle French, *piquant* meant "stimulating" or "irritating." By the seventeenth century it had come to refer particularly to food.

MAKE IT STICK:

Write a short description using the following: *piquancy, tennis, December, flurries,* and *Marilyn.*

LYCANTHROPE
(LIE-kan-thrope), noun

A werewolf.

MAKE IT STICK:

Using the word *lycanthrope,* write a short scene or paragraph describing one entering a clearing.

TRIVIA:

While the first lycanthropes were mentioned in Europe in 60 C.E., the English term, derived from the Greek *lykanthrōpos,* literally "wolf-man," didn't come along until the late 1500s, referring to a mentally ill person who believed he was a wolf. In 1825, the term morphed to mean "a human who supernaturally transforms into a wolf." Modern-day beliefs are that lycanthropes are more human-looking in nature than werewolves and can transform into their lycanthropic form at any time, not just during a full moon.

VENAL

(VEE-nul), adjective

Corruptible or excessively devoted to selfish interests (as opposed to public interests); susceptible to bribes.

MAKE IT STICK:

Write a scene from the Prohibition era using the following:
venal, *boss*, *motorboat*, and *shed*.

PIXIE

(PIK-see), noun

An elf or fairy.

EXAMPLE:

The villages believed the mysterious theft to be the work of mischievous **PIXIES** and trolls.

TRIVIA:

The Pixie Day legend states that when a local bishop commissioned a set of bells for a new church in Ottery St. Mary, England, the pixies were worried the bells would signal the end of their rule over the land. They tried, unsuccessfully, to thwart the bishop's efforts. Pixie Day commemorates the banishment of the pixies from the town to a local cave known as Pixies' Parlour.

MAKE IT STICK:

Write your very own Shakespeare scene incorporating a mischievous *pixie*.

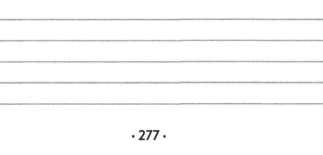

INDEFATIGABLE
(in-de-FAH-ti-gu-bul), adjective

Stubbornly obstinate in pursuit of a particular goal.

TRIVIA:

The first use is in the late sixteenth century and it derives from the Latin *indefatigabilis*. At some point there seems to have been a counterword—*defatigable*—but it died out sometime after the eighteenth century.

MAKE IT STICK:

Write a scene incorporating *indefatigable*, *Barry*, *mountain*, and *baggage*.

MUSS

(muss), verb

To tousle or dishevel.

EXAMPLE:

Lynne admired the model's **MUSSED** hair but knew that what looked sexy on a long, elegant face would look like an accident with a blender on her.

TRIVIA:

From the nineteenth century, a variant of *mess*. In Stanley Kubrick's film *Dr. Strangelove*, the war-mongering General Buck Turgidson, urging the US president to undertake a nuclear first strike on the Soviet Union, is questioned about Soviet retaliation. "I'm not saying we wouldn't get our hair mussed. But I do say no more than ten to twenty million killed, tops. Uh, depending on the breaks."

MAKE IT STICK:

Finish this sentence using *muss*: Lily, dressed for a night out with her pals, stopped short when she saw her crazy Aunt Hilda sitting on the living room sofa...

APPROBATION
(aa-pro-BAY-shun), noun

Honor or accolades.

EXAMPLE:

The **APPROBATION** he received for his first novel was nothing compared to the glowing reviews that greeted his second.

TRIVIA:

This word is from the Old French *apro-bacion*, which got it (naturally!) from the Latin *approbationem*, meaning "approval." The *probus* part of the root means "to prove" or "honest."

MAKE IT STICK:

Give yourself some *approbation*!

TROUPER
(TROO-pur), noun

An actor, especially a veteran performer who is able to come through no matter what; any person who is remarkably dependable.

EXAMPLE:

Nancy drove through a snowstorm to run the desk on Saturday— what a **TROUPER**!

TRIVIA:

Mamma Mia! Here We Go Again director Ol Parker says the "Super Trouper" scene at the end of the move looks like fun because it *was* fun. "We played the song loudly and sent them off to different corners....They just had an absolute hoot."

MAKE IT STICK:

Write a sentence that includes your best friend and the word *trouper*.

WANDERLUST
(WAN-dur-lust), noun

A strong, innate desire to travel.

EXAMPLE:

While Jerry told his family each Thanksgiving that he would someday settle down and raise a family, his irrepressible **WANDERLUST** kept him from putting down roots until he was well into his sixties.

TRIVIA:

Author Upton Sinclair wrote of his character Jurgis from his 1906 novel *The Jungle*, "The old wanderlust had gotten into his blood, the joy of the unbound life, the joy of seeking, of hoping without limit."

MAKE IT STICK:

Finish this scene using the word *wanderlust*:
Hoyt and N.J. never stayed in one place for too long...

_____

_____

_____

_____

_____

_____

_____

_____

_____

_____

_____

_____

ATAVISTIC
(at-uh-VIS-tic), adjective

Having characteristics regressing to a more primitive type;
resembling a distant relative.

TRIVIA:

Thought to have been coined by French botanist Antoine Nicolas Duchesne in the early 1800s, *atavistic* was initially a biology term. There are many natural atavistic traits animals and organisms carry with them for hundreds or thousands of years.

MAKE IT STICK:

Describe a scene in which an animal or human character
is behaving in an *atavistic* way.

_____

_____

_____

_____

_____

_____

_____

_____

_____

_____

_____

_____

_____

TOTTER

(TOT-tur), verb

To walk or move with unsteady steps; to sway at ground level.

EXAMPLE:

The sight of Mr. Bass **TOTTERING** home from another night at Mulvaney's Pub was enough to make a teetotaler out of anyone.

TRIVIA:

Many things can cause you to totter, including the exhausting job of parenting! In an episode of *I Love Lucy*, Lucy recounts to her husband her day spent chasing after their son: "He chases the pigeons. I chase after him. He runs after the squirrels. I run after him….We go on the teeter-totter. He teeters, I totter."

MAKE IT STICK:

Finish the scene, incorporating *totter*: Mike and Vickie were packed inside Pat O'Brien's trying to get the bartender's attention. "Two hurricanes to go!" Mike yelled when he finally caught her eye. As soon as they got their drinks they headed for the door, hoping they hadn't missed the start of the Mardi Gras parade...

NOSTRUM
(NAH-strum), noun

Something meant to be used for medicinal purposes;
more broadly, a cure for something.

EXAMPLE:

The politician, from the platform, issued a series of **NOSTRUMS** for the ills plaguing the country.

TRIVIA:

This word had entered common usage by the seventeenth century and comes from the Latin phrase *nostrum remedium*, meaning "our remedy."

MAKE IT STICK:

Write a paragraph using *nostrum, peddler, wagon,* and *donkey*.

ANFRACTUOUS

(an-FRACK-chuh-wuss),
adjective

Full of windings and intricacies.

EXAMPLE:

The **ANFRACTUOUS** plot of the recent spy movie turned me off so much that I don't intend to see the film's sequel.

TRIVIA:

Originally from Latin and first used in English in the 1620s, T.S. Eliot used *anfractuous* in the French sense (meaning "craggy") when he wrote, "Paint me the bold anfractuous rocks/Faced by the snarled and yelping seas."

MAKE IT STICK:

Incorporating the word *anfractuous,* write about a novel or movie you've seen recently that had a convoluted plot.

_____
_____
_____
_____
_____
_____
_____
_____

ENVISAGE

(en-VIH-zaj), verb

To imagine or foresee something.

EXAMPLE:

Ray **ENVISAGED** a time when his financial worries would be over.

TRIVIA:

From the French meaning "to look in the face of." Many people have envisaged great things; the problem is making them come true.

MAKE IT STICK:

Write a sentence using *envisage* in which an urban planner is trying to convince a city's political leaders of something.

_____
_____
_____
_____
_____
_____
_____
_____

LUMINARY
(LOO-mih-nay-ree), noun

Something that emits light; a person widely renowned
and respected in his or her area of expertise.

EXAMPLE:

Other **LUMINARIES** who attended the party included the author of this year's Pulitzer Prize winner for drama.

TRIVIA:

Luminary came to English around the mid-1400s by way of the twelfth-century Anglo-French *luminarie*, meaning "lamp, lighting." The Latin word *lumen* means "light," a term used today to denote the quantity of visible light emitted by a light bulb.

MAKE IT STICK:

Describe a winter scene incorporating *luminaries*.

VISCERAL
(VISS-er-ul), adjective

Deeply felt. Literally, from the viscera (bodily interior).

MAKE IT STICK:

Using the word *visceral*, write about a time you felt something very deeply.

TRIVIA:

The 2003 documentary *Failure Is Not an Option* (whose title came from the phrase spoken by flight director Gene Kranz in the film *Apollo 13*) notes the mission to land men on the moon after JFK's assassination became a crusade: "This was now our mission to win this battle, for President Kennedy. It was visceral, it was gut, we are going to do it, and we're the right people to do it, and we're going to do it in the time frame he said we'll do it."

ABOUT THE AUTHOR

Francine Puckly is a freelance writer/editor who covers a wide range of topics from her home in Massachusetts. She also writes young adult contemporary and historical fiction and is cofounder of 24CarrotWriting.com. She holds two degrees from Cornell University.